THE WAY OF JESUS

COMPASSION
in PRACTICE

—

Frank Rogers Jr.

UPPER
ROOM BOOKS®
NASHVILLE

Cover and interior design: Faceout Studio / faceoutstudio.com

Library of Congress Cataloging-in-Publication Data

Names: Rogers, Frank, 1958– author.
Title: Compassion in practice : the way of Jesus / Frank Rogers Jr.
Description: Nashville : Upper Room Books, 2016.
Identifiers: LCCN 2016006367| ISBN 9780835815666 (print) | ISBN 9780835815673 (mobi) | ISBN 9780835815680 (epub)
Subjects: LCSH: Compassion—Religious aspects—Christianity.
Classification: LCC BV4647.S9 R645 2016 | DDC 241/.4—dc23
LC record available at https://lccn.loc.gov/2016006367

CONTENTS

EXERCISES

Acknowledgments

The Compassion Practice would not exist without the exacting insight, tireless devotion, and selfless giving of Mark Yaconelli and Andy Dreitcer. You both have as incisive a barometer of spiritual vitality as anyone I know. I am forever grateful for your belief in this work and your dedication to its flourishing. Your generosity brought the pulse to life.

The teachings and practices of this book were developed and refined through the Triptykos School of Compassion at the Center for Engaged Compassion. In addition to Mark and Andy, I am ever indebted to the staff and participants who have journeyed along this radical spiritual path: Cate Wilson, Jenn Hooten and, before them, Steve and Krystalynn Martin—staff who transform organizational details into compassionate artistry; Nancy Linton—our sage and spiritual director; Alane Daugherty, Cate, Jenn, Doug Frank, Karri Backer, Rachel Fox, Samantha Lynne Gupta, Greta Ronningen, Jeff Hayes, Steffani Kizziar, Holly Cordone, Mary Pierce, Leslie Adams, Anny Genato, Blanca Bañuelos, Sarah Dornbos, Dennis Sheridan, Nancy Fowler, Tim Feak, Seth Schoen, Carol Amor, Donna Farrell, David Okonkwo, Kathy Welch, and Ricki Ladekarl—coleaders, facilitators, and teachers of the curriculum whose insights and passion bring clarity and inspiration; and Don Morrison of the Morrison Foundation whose generous support launched the school in the first place.

The Center for Engaged Compassion is housed at Claremont School of Theology (CST). I am grateful to President Jeffrey Kah-Jin Kuan, Dean Sheryl Kujawa-Holbrook, and all the administrative staff who have unequivocally supported the center's work. I am also grateful to the hundreds of students, retreatants, contemplative practitioners, social activists, and spiritual seekers who have given themselves to this work in seminary classes, weeklong retreats, pilot programs, healing and reconciliation workshops, and various compassion formation offerings through Triptykos and CST.

Your commitment to personal healing and social transformation sustains my work and gives me hope for the world.

Loved ones, friends, and colleagues read drafts of the manuscript: Mark, Andy, Doug, Nancy, Alane, Ulrike Guthrie, Jim Neafsey, Daniel Judah Sklar, Philip Clayton, Tom Rogers, and Justin Rogers—thank you for your wisdom and unwavering support. Cate, thank you for the great job you did on the Leader's Guide. And from the beginning, the Upper Room staff has tended this book with care, skill, and generosity: Jeannie Crawford-Lee, John Mogabgab, Joanna Bradley, Jeremy Bakker, Sharon Conley, Anne Trudel, and Johnny Sears—this book could not have found a better home.

Finally, my family holds me in the compassion that I teach. Alane, Justin, Michael, and Sammy, you are my teachers, my inspiration, the ground that steadies and restores me. Alane, you are love; you are compassion in practice.

In the fall of 2015, Alane's mother, Sandy Ferguson, passed away at eighty-eight. Through her last days, her five children and their partners surrounded her—a circle of love that cradled her final moments and released her into the cosmic source of all compassion. That circle of compassion embodies all that this book teaches. That circle holds blood relatives and in-laws, laughter and tears, daytime dancing and nighttime vigils, life and death. It is a sacred circle in which we glimpse God's loving presence that encircles every particle of creation. Alane sat at the head of that circle, at the head of her mother's bed, companioning her mom a few steps into death while tethered to her loved ones here. Babe, this book is for you, for your mom, and for the circle of care with which you hold me, our family, and our planet with hands outstretched into this world and the next.

Jesus' Spiritual Path
of Compassion

When my son, Justin, was four years old, he and I found ourselves stumbling through life confined within a one-room apartment. We were snug. We shared a bedroom, we squeezed into a single stuffed chair, and the coffee table doubled as a writing desk and Lego station. But we got by. When our close friends—a family of four that included my young godson, Jackson—moved to southern California, I agreed to let them stay in our apartment until they closed on the house they were buying. This arrangement seemed fine when I thought it would only be a couple of days. Soon, "a couple of days" turned into a week, one week turned into two, two turned into three, and so on. For a solid month, six people crowded into a space that had felt cramped with only two. Justin suffered the worst. He had to give up his bed; sleep on the floor with his dad; share his toys, his videos, and his father, for that matter. But he hung in there the best that he could.

Until one day, Justin had just had it.

The sliding glass door in the apartment opened onto a mound of dirt where kids throughout the complex gathered to play. Justin had a shovel and was digging up a boulder—what he claimed was the jawbone of a Tyrannosaurus rex. A kid from the neighborhood, wanting the shovel, came over to Justin and grabbed it. Justin grabbed back. A tug-of-war ensued with each boy pulling and pushing until the neighbor kid freed the spade with a final yank that brought Justin to his knees. Justin stood up, gave the kid a look that could kill, then kicked the dirt, stomped down the mound, slammed his way through the sliding glass door, stormed through the living room, and slouched into his corner rocking chair where he folded his arms and scowled.

"What's the matter?" I asked him.

"I'm mad," he said. "I'm never playing with my friends ever again in my entire life." I nodded knowingly and let him sit it out.

My godson, Jackson, was oblivious to the scene. Also four years old, he was playing Legos on the coffee table with the radio on behind him. After a commercial break, a song drifted forth from the speakers. It was one of those songs—a Kenny G saxophone solo—that wraps itself around us, seeps into our bones, and induces us to tap our toes before we even are aware we are doing it. The song worked its magic on Jackson. The young boy bobbed his head and rocked his shoulders until, unable to constrain himself any longer, he leaped up from his Legos and started dancing in the middle of the living room. Bopping to the music, he looked toward the corner and said, "Hey Justin, you want to dance with me?" Justin stared for a moment and then replied, "Sure, why not?" And he popped up and joined in the dance with Jackson.

For the next several minutes, the two of them were giddy. They do-si-doed, twirled, and shuffled; they twisted and skipped like some slapstick combination of Fred Astaire, John Travolta, and the Three Stooges taking on an Argentinean tango. They were lit up—giggling and squealing as if drunk on life, so drunk that, when the song ended, Jackson turned to Justin and said, "Hey, you want to go out and dig for dinosaur bones?" To which Justin replied, "Sure, let's go."

Justin and Jackson were halfway out the sliding glass door before I could get their attention. "Justin," I said, "where are you going?"

"I'm going out to play with my friends," he answered.

"I thought you were never going to play with your friends ever again in your entire life."

He looked at me like he didn't know what I was talking about. Then his words came back to him, as if a lifetime ago.

"Oh yeah," he said. "You know, I think the dancing took my mad away."

————————

Wherever we turn, our mad rips our world apart. It tears us up through terrorist bombings and retaliatory attacks, school shootings and playground bullying, domestic abuse, gangland killings, and even molestations in our sacred institutions. Violence, racism, and poverty stalk our streets and ravage our families. Our madness knows no limits. And its blows can be brutal.

Our mad infects our relationships as well. Between loved ones at home, colleagues at the workplace, and adversaries dissenting in our political spaces, we witness cycles of rage, resentment, blame, and dismissiveness that erode the very bonds on which love and community depend. Our mad eats at us from the inside out. Fear, disgust, anger, despair, spite, shame, and loathing of others and ourselves consume us with such savage ferocity that we are either possessed by their powers or resistant to their grip through numbing and self-medication. We are a world at war, and the war is waged both within and without.

And yet.

In the midst of the violence that rages around us, music moves through our world as well. This music flows from the very heartbeat of God at the sacred center of the cosmos, and it whispers through every sphere of the universe, inviting each person, each particle of creation, to move in harmony with its restorative rhythms. Contemplative Christians call this music the song of creation, the cosmic dance of the Divine, the symphony of life in which each soul is a single, lyrical strand.[1] The music is the Holy Spirit—a melody of life, love, peace, personal power, grace, and justice. It offers a reconciled connectedness that extends to all without exception. The song never stops playing. No violence can slay it, no despair can silence it, and no frantic din or maddening fury can drive it away entirely. We are within it; it is within us. It beats in the depths of our soul.

Mystics hear this music in their silence. Children who dance amidst living room Legos hear it in their play. Prophets of nonviolence from Cape Town to Birmingham have picked up its echo beating for freedom in oppressive lands. And they all bear witness. As we listen for its sustaining presence, even in conflict most severe, and as we give ourselves over to its redemptive rhythms ever aching to receive us, we find that the beat does take hold. In the mire of our mad, a grace at the source of our suffering meets us. We are restored to our essence of love and vitality, and we move to partner with the sacred presence resuscitating life within our wounded world. In short, we find ourselves dancing in time with the Divine. And that dancing—just as Justin said—takes our mad away.

The Christian Call of Compassion

Spiritual traditions throughout the world recognize the music's sacred essence. They call this essence *compassion*. "All faiths," writes Karen Armstrong, a noted scholar of religion, "insist that compassion is the test of true spirituality and that it brings us into relation with the transcendence we call God, Brahman, Nirvana, or Dao."[2] As Armstrong's Charter for Compassion reminds us, some version of the Golden Rule lies at the heart of every religious tradition. In fact, the ethic of compassion—to do unto others as we would have them do unto us—is the essential summation of any religion's core and vital truth. A famous Talmudic tale provides an illustration. As legend has it, a pagan once approached the great sage Hillel and promised to convert to Judaism if Hillel could recite the entire Torah while standing on one leg. Hillel was up to the challenge. He responded simply, "What is hateful to yourself, do not do to another. That is the whole Torah. The rest is but commentary."[3]

Religions promote compassion. All else is commentary. When true to their spiritual essence, religious traditions do no more than deepen people's connection to the compassionate source of life, restore people to the fullness of love and loving vitality, and send people forth with expanded capacities to be active embodiments of compassion in the world. This is the heartbeat of any religion that is truly spiritually alive—its communities, teachings, and practices beat with the pulse of compassion, and it nurtures the pulse of compassion within the heartbeat of its followers. Quite simply, religious traditions are meant to be spiritual paths of transformative love. They are called to be schools of compassion.

Christianity is no exception. Its vital essence lies not in being a religion but in creating a spiritual path, and the spiritual path that it maps out is one of transformative compassion.

Now, to suggest that Christianity is less a religion and more a spiritual path of compassion demands critical scrutiny. For one thing, religions are constituted by religious forms—sacred writings, liturgical practices, codes of conduct, and the like—and Christianity is as laden with religious forms as any other religion. Christianity includes institutions to belong to, creeds to believe in, commandments to obey, doctrines to espouse, clerics to esteem, texts to internalize, and rituals to practice with steadfast routine. Often these forms become ends in themselves—their observance demanded regardless of how wooden or rote they have become. Anthony de Mello, SJ, an Indian Jesuit priest, compares this to visiting a restaurant and eating the cardboard menu.[4]

We should not confuse religious forms with the palpable presence of God. Forms may contain that presence, mediate that presence, bear witness to that presence, but the forms themselves provide a feeble substitute for the living reality of God. As Sandra Lommasson conceives of them, religious forms are similar to the ring of stones that encircle a sacred fire.[5] Stones can shelter a fire, even intensify its warmth and enhance its strength, but stones grow cold if the fire within dissolves into cinders. The stones of Christian religious forms are as vulnerable to such coldness as any other ring of religious stones.

More troubling, however, is the tragic truth that these stones have often been used to bruise and batter. The shadow side of Christianity has contributed as much violence to our world as it has peace and compassion. Throughout history, wars have been waged and territories raped in the bloody spread of the gospel. Muslims and Jews, women and witches, gays and pagans, the divorced, the unorthodox, the sexually active, and the sexually abused have all been burned on the sinister stakes of Christian intolerance. Church teachings and spiritual practices have demonized our emotions, bodies, passions, depressions, hungers, urges, egos, doubts, and pride while feeding the shame-filled self-loathing that has ravaged innumerable souls. And through it all, ecclesiastical hierarchies, communities of faith, and families of Christian conviction have all too often silenced dissent, demanded obedience, required conformity, and exacted fidelity in unyielding and scarring alliance with the Christ they have created. If Christianity is a spiritual path of compassion, this path has sometimes been very well concealed.

Nevertheless, the heartbeat at the core of Christian spirituality pulsates with compassion. This beat began with the spiritual teacher who inaugurated this path in the first place. Jesus never founded a religion. Strictly speaking, he was not even Christian. He was a Jewish mystic, an itinerant rabbi, and a social prophet much like Jeremiah before him or Martin Luther King Jr., who later followed in his footsteps. To be sure, Jesus' followers—on Easter and beyond—experienced a risen Christ, a living and eternal presence across time and space. Yet, that risen Christ was the living presence of a very particular man, and that presence only confirmed and sustained that man's historical teachings.

And this man Jesus was decidedly Jewish. He attended the synagogue and observed the faithful practices of having a bar mitzvah and reciting the Shema daily. He absorbed the stories of Moses, Elijah, holy men, and liberators, and he studied the law and the prophets. He kept the sabbath, taught the Torah, celebrated Passover, and made pilgrimage to Jerusalem. To his death, Jesus remained unwaveringly devoted to the faith of his people. Yes, he exposed hypocrisy, critiqued abuse, and encouraged radical renewal, but his teachings and practices were rooted in the living essence of the faith to which he passionately committed himself.

Jesus was also Jewish within a very specific historical context. Jesus was a poor peasant within a brutally occupied land. This occupation possessed political, economic, and ecclesiastical dimensions. Politically speaking, Palestine was a conquered territory. A strategic trade and travel corridor within the Roman Empire, the country was ruled by Roman proxies—Pontius Pilate, for example—and garrisons of ever-present Roman centurions. The Roman governor maintained order through Jewish aristocratic rulers, such as Herod the Great, who lived in obscene luxury in exchange for their service to the Roman Empire. These Jewish rulers were ruthless in their own right. One was so debased that as an orgy gift to an exotic dancer, he had John the Baptist, the mentor who baptized Jesus, beheaded.

Economically speaking, the peasant class of Palestine—90 percent of the population—paid the price for keeping peace with the Empire and maintaining the opulence of the aristocratic elite. Taxation—severe beyond human endurance—generated so much resentment that tax collectors, though fellow townspeople, became social pariahs. When farmland fell into foreclosure, absentee landlords seized it. Indentured servants, day laborers, and people encumbered by impossible debt so populated the countryside that their plight was immediately recognizable to those who heard Jesus' parables.

Ecclesiastically speaking, corruption ran rampant throughout the religious hierarchy in Jerusalem. The high priest and his judicial council, called the Sanhedrin, became political bedfellows with Roman authorities. In exchange for maintaining civil order and guaranteeing the steady flow of taxation revenue, these ruling clerics were allowed to amass large holdings of land, wield virtually unchecked jurisdictional power, and maintain a religious stranglehold on the Jewish population.

Cultic purity was mandatory. If deemed impure, a person was banned from any house of worship, from any civil assembly, and from sitting at a table for food and fellowship in any Jewish home. This purity was secured through sacrifices at the Temple, either in person or by proxy. Temple taxes for sacrificial offerings were obscenely excessive, and the profits were siphoned to support the luxuries of the ecclesiastical elite. The Temple itself—the sacred center of Jewish worship and the site of the Holy of Holies—became a symbol of religious extortion and imperial collaboration. The house of prayer, as Jesus decried, became a den of robbers.

Within this land of military occupation, economic depression, and religious exploitation, Jesus traveled from town to town and gathered the people, healed the wounded, and shared a message that brought hope to the hopeless. All who encountered him recognized that something was special about this man. He had a presence about him, the aura of a man on intimate terms with God. He had a kindness about him, an understanding for the plight of the suffering and a care for the weak and discarded. He had an authority about him, an inner wisdom as present while debating with the religious experts as when illuminating the scriptures through stories to the poor. Clearly this man knew a way of sustaining life within the system of death that surrounded him. He knew how to live in harmony with God apart from the snares of the religious structures. He knew how to claim dignity and power in the midst of forces that try to deaden and dehumanize. He knew how to practice peace within the violence of an oppressive society.

In short, Jesus was a spiritual teacher. Like Buddha or Lao Tzu or Mohammed, he taught a path of transformation—a means, at once personal, political, internal, and external, through which people may live vitally connected to God. This way of life most characterized those who pledge allegiance to Jesus; indeed his earliest disciples, after his death, were known not as *Christians* but as *followers of the Way*.

The *Way* that Jesus taught is radical, both in the sense of its rising from the deepest taproot of his tradition and in its scandalous upending of the foundational assumptions on which an entire system of oppression was based. It offered a radical understanding of an extravagantly loving God and how such a God could be known; it promoted a radical sense of human dignity and a capacity for emboldened and abundant life; and it cultivated an ethic of radical care that extended not only to loved ones, neighbors, and strangers but also to enemies, opponents, and oppressors. This path of Jesus—summed up as loving God with every dimension of our being, cultivating an authentic love for ourselves, and loving our neighbors as ourselves—was, at its core, a way of radical compassion.

Loving God: A Radically Compassionate Sacred Source

God's heart beats with the pulse of compassion. God's heart is not hardened toward the plight of the world; it is not callous and cold in the face of suffering. In fact, hard-heartedness, like that of Pharaoh before the Jews in Egypt, is the chief characteristic of those who are ungodly. God's heart is moist. It is moved by the cries of those who suffer, and it delights in the beauty of creation's flourishing. In stark contrast to the God espoused by the religious authorities—a God who is quick to condemn and whose purity is so severely holy it refuses to be stained by human imperfection—Jesus likens God to an extravagantly loving father who grieves a prodigal's plunge through the pig sties of obscenity, who suffers with the pain of separation, and who rushes down the road, eyes wet with compassion, to embrace his beloved's return, soiled clothing and all. (See Luke 15:11-32.) Like the rain that falls on the unjust and the just, the sun that shines on the good and the evil, God's compassion remains ever-present, abundant, and unequivocally extended to all without exception—the elder as well as the prodigal, the Republican as well as the Democrat, the Muslim as well as the Christian, the terrorist as well as the victim pulled from the wreckage.

Some years ago, a college student boarded a bus, heading home for spring break. Because the bus was nearly full, he sat down next to a man staring out the window. The man was middle-aged and dressed in denim. He bore the hard-edged look of someone haunted by a life he would rather soon forget. The man was not up for small talk. He was lost in himself. He simply gazed at the passing cornfields and farmhouses as the bus rolled along the two-lane country roads.

A couple of hours into the ride, the hard-edged man grew agitated. Fingering his work cap, he stared down at the floor, only casting quick glances out the window as if not wanting to look too long. The college student asked if the man was okay. The man regarded him, glanced once more out the window, then desperately shared his tale.

"Twenty years ago," the man confessed, "I killed a man. I was boozin' it up, got inside a car, never saw the guy just crossing the street. I've been in prison all these years just thinkin' about it. I felt so ashamed. I sent a letter to my folks—told 'em that I knew I wasn't any good and that I was in prison, but I didn't tell 'em where. As far as they were concerned, they should count me dead. I haven't seen or heard from 'em ever since.

"I got paroled a couple days ago. Didn't have no place to go really. So I wrote my folks. I told 'em I was getting out. And I know I've brought nothing but shame to them and our family, but I told 'em if they would have me, I would love to come home. I'd get it if they didn't want me back. So I'd make it easy on 'em. In our front yard is this big, old oak tree. The bus drives right by our house on the way into town. If they would have me, all they got to do is tie a yellow ribbon around that tree. If it's there, I'll get off the bus at town and come home. If it's not there, I'll just stay on the bus. And they don't ever have to lay eyes on me again.

"The thing is, now that we're getting close, I'm not sure I can bear to look. I mean, I get it. But if that oak tree is bare, why, I don't know what I'll do."

The man started to look out the window then stopped himself, staring at the floor instead. Then an idea came to him.

"Say," he asked the student, "would you mind looking for me? I'll just look the other way, and you can let me know."

The student agreed, and the man swapped seats with him. The student scouted while the ex-con fingered his cap and stared at the floor. House after house passed by. Tree after tree was barren of ribbons. The bus drove closer to the town.

Then, with a shout, the student saw it. "Oh my God, you have to see this!"

The ex-con dared to look as the bus was passing his childhood home. A giant oak tree stood sentry in the yard. The tree did not bear a single yellow ribbon; it boasted hundreds of them. Flapping in the breeze from every branch of the tree, an explosion of yellow ribbons proclaimed to the world, "Our boy is coming home. And we cannot wait to embrace him."

———————

Those ribbons serve as a parable of the God that Jesus knows. His God is extravagantly compassionate, with a love so wide it welcomes home every lost and broken wanderer of the world. In fact, compassion so thoroughly captures God's essence that Jesus rewords the core commandment that formed the central pillar in the purity code of his day. With brilliant precision, he substitutes, "You shall be holy to me; for I the LORD am holy" (Lev. 20:26) with his own summative invitation, "Be compassionate just as your Father in heaven is compassionate" (Luke 6:36, AP). At the very core of God's identity, we find neither judgment, punishment, cold aloofness, nor unapproachable strictness;

rather, God welcomes us into the embrace of God's loving presence—a presence that is infinitely understanding about our shames and our pain and only too eager to adorn us in robes and rings of glory.

And yet, scandalously, Jesus goes further. We can know this God of extravagant compassion directly. Jesus' own spiritual journey is grounded in an immediate experience of God at his baptism. God communicates directly to him: "You are my Son, the Beloved; with you I am well pleased" (Mark 1:11). And Jesus knows that this same God yearns for all persons to come to know their own belovedness and know it within every cell of their being—with all of their heart and soul and mind and strength. Jesus' understanding of God is remarkable within a system where the religious elite have the power to make spiritual purity, cultic cleanliness, and righteousness before God dependent upon paying Temple taxes, fulfilling codes of holiness, and securing ecclesiastical pardon for ever-evolving offenses. Jesus proclaims that we are already held in God's compassionate embrace, we are already acceptable in God's sight. God has already forgiven our sins, and the forgiveness has nothing to do with eating clean food, fulfilling holy days of obligation, or paying off those set out to exploit us with blood sacrifice. It has only to do with opening our eyes, waking up to that which is already and eternally true, and allowing the reality of God's infinite love to settle deep within us. We can know in the core of our beings that a compassionate God holds us with care, and we can know it with such an inner authority that we can be free from the insidious power of any body—religious or otherwise—that seeks to coerce our acquiescence.

Loving Ourselves: Radical Compassion Extended Within

Jesus seeks to restore personhood, not diminish it. The spiritual path he teaches empowers human dignity, emboldens abundant vitality, and cultivates a flourishing as radiant as the lilies of the field in full blossom. Jesus proclaims, "I came that they may have life, and have it abundantly" (John 10:10). Such restorative vitality flows from God's abundant compassion. As surely as our suffering moves God, God beams with delight when we shine in the fullness of our power and giftedness. When we use our gifts, claim our power, find our voice, or own our dignity, God cheers for us. "That's my girl," the voice from the heavens champions. "That's my boy. That's my beloved in whom I am well pleased."

Our timidity, our powerlessness, our shame, and our diminishment bring no pleasure to God. On the contrary, God seeks to free us from all that mars our nobility in order to liberate us from the lacerations of self-judgment, the humiliations of shame, and the subservience to domination that dim the radiance of our beauty and giftedness. "The glory of God is humanity fully alive," Saint Irenaeus attests. God aches for our flourishing and aches to be our greatest enthusiast.

To Jesus, fully alive human beings resemble the living essence of God. God made us in God's image, fashioned from a sacred blueprint. To the extent that God's essence is compassion, our essence, likewise, is compassion. When we are most true to ourselves, most in harmony with our created essence, we mirror the very likeness of God. Rooted and restored in God's love and delight, we become persons of emboldened compassion.

This compassion includes a compassion for ourselves. Within Christian traditions, self-compassion has been underemphasized and sometimes outright subverted. While we laud the Christian mandate of loving our neighbor, some people regard self-love with suspicion. They believe delighting in ourselves to be an offense and tending to our needs before those of others to be outrageously sacrilegious. Still, Jesus invites us to love our neighbor *as* ourselves, not *instead of* ourselves. The care, goodwill, and delight we extend to ourselves should be the measure of that which we offer to others. For some, this sets a rather low bar.

We do not love ourselves well. Self-loathing, self-disgust, and self-castigation are obscenely epidemic. We internally berate ourselves, *You stupid idiot. How could you do such a shameful thing? If people ever saw what you are really like, they would turn away in disgust.* If we attacked others with the words with which we attack ourselves, people would rightly consider our actions abusive. Self-denigration is assaultive; furthermore, it is blasphemous. God beholds us with sacred compassion. We bear the illustrious lineage of being the offspring of the Divine. God holds our shames with infinite understanding and delights in our bliss with unfettered enthusiasm. To see ourselves differently from the way in which God sees us is the very definition of self-deception. And it violates the teachings of Jesus.

Jesus offers an antidote to self-hatred, not a poison to feed its corrosiveness. His spiritual path invites us into a relationship with ourselves marked by the compassion with which God relates to us. Self-compassion does not hold our shadows, shames, and transgressions with condemnation and disgust but with the understanding and care that heals and restores. Self-compassion cultivates the personal power necessary to claim our dignity, even in the face of forces that threaten to dehumanize us, and it savors our beauty when we use and celebrate our gifts. Out of the abundance of self-compassion rooted in God's compassion for us, we can have genuine compassion for others. Indeed, this is the only way through which we can love our neighbors—with the very same love that we love ourselves.

Loving Our Neighbors: Radical Compassion Extended to Others

While the spiritual path Jesus teaches includes an invitation to know our compassionate God more deeply and to cultivate a love for ourselves, it also bears decidedly social and political dimensions. Jesus is not only a mystic and a spiritual teacher but also a peacemaker and a prophet of social transformation within a violent and oppressive society. And in those arenas as well, radical compassion informs his teaching.

Jesus advocates the coming of the kin-dom of God.[6] Whatever its otherworldly dimensions, for Jesus the kin-dom of God very much includes becoming embodied "on earth as it is in heaven." God's kin-dom is how the world would be governed if God were king instead of Caesar, Herod, the high priest, the rich, the city elite, the racially entitled, or any other person or entity of privilege that rises to power and influence. God's kin-dom reflects the character and essence of God. As such, it embodies what Marcus Borg calls "the politics of compassion."[7]

The politics of compassion are, first, radically inclusive. Like the sun and the rain whose reach extends without discrimination, the kin-dom of God welcomes everyone. Jesus embodies this inclusiveness through the central cultural custom of his day: the practice of table fellowship. In the ancient Jewish world, only the cultically clean are allowed to dine at a ritually pure household. At Jesus' table, however, the invitation is sent to all—the sick, the lame, lepers, prostitutes, tax collectors, traitors, outcasts, and centurions.

The politics of compassion also promote a kin-dom of justice. Like the Beloved Community about which Martin Luther King Jr. dared to dream, Jesus envisions a kin-dom in which the oppressed are liberated, the falsely imprisoned set free, the victims of violence safe and empowered, the brutal weapons of perpetrators dismantled, the poor fed, wealth shared, the wounded healed, and the estranged reconciled with forgiveness and accountability. This vision evokes the poetic metaphors of the lion lying down with the lamb, swords being beaten into plowshares, and deserts blooming with enough vegetation to feed the entire world. In this vision, even the most savagely hostile persons find their way to peace. Jesus devotes his life to this vision, even to the point of death.

I remember when the radicality of this vision hit home for me personally. Justin was three when his mom and I divorced. Shortly thereafter, during Mass at our local Catholic church, Justin asked why he could not have Eucharist like everyone else at church.

I went to the priest.

I told the priest that Justin, now more than ever, needed to feel at home in his religious community, that Jesus certainly welcomed the children at the table, and that I considered it more than appropriate for Justin to begin his sacramental preparation. I also assured the priest that as a seminary professor in spiritual formation, I would take personal responsibility for Justin learning the meaning of Eucharist and how to partake of it in a responsible manner. In the meantime, while I prepared him for the church-sanctioned ceremony, I would break a small piece from the host given to me and share it with Justin until the church ceremony when he could receive a full host for himself.

The priest agreed, and Justin and I established a sacramental routine. Every Sunday, as we drove to church, I would share another story, another insight, another dimension of what Eucharist means to Christians. Justin would take in my words, and during Communion, I would break off a small piece of my host and share it with my boy.

After some months of this routine, I began to ponder additional lessons to impart to Justin when something occurred to me that I had not yet described.

"Justin," I said on the car ride to church, "there's another reason why we take Eucharist each week. When Jesus comes back, there's going to be a huge party—the biggest party you could possibly imagine. It'll be called the feast of life. And what's really cool about this party is that everyone in the world is invited—not just friends and family but strangers too. We'll all be at the same party—even people from different schools will be at the same party, even people from different countries will be at the same party, even"—and now I suggested something outrageous, "people who are enemies to each other, even they will be at the same party. But they will be friends, eating bread and drinking wine and celebrating the feast of life together. Isn't that cool?"

Justin pondered this a while, stretching his imagination into so vast a hope. Then he wanted to make sure he got it right.

"So you're telling me," he said, "at the feast of life, even enemies are going to be friends again?"

"Yeah, Justin, even enemies will be friends."

"So, at the feast of life, even the coyote and the roadrunner will be friends?"

"Yeah," I smiled. He got it. "Even the coyote and the roadrunner will be friends."

"Even Dorothy and the witch will be friends?"

"Yes, even Dorothy and the witch will be friends."

His vision stretched as far as it dared. Then it dared to stretch even further.

"Dad?"

"Yeah, Justin."

"At the feast of life, will even you and Mommy be friends?"

His hope pierced my heart like a spear. But I knew what to say. "Yes, Justin, at the feast of life, even your mom and I will be friends once more."

He took this in. Then he turned his hope into sacrament. "Daddy," he said, "at Eucharist today, this time, I want the big piece."

———————

Jesus dreams of a kin-dom radical in its inclusivity and in the reach of its restoration. In addition, the means by which Jesus advances this kin-dom are thoroughly counterintuitive. Jesus urges his followers to build this kin-dom through a nonviolent ethic of extraordinary compassion. This ethic of compassion certainly entails loving our neighbor as ourselves—doing unto others what we would have them do unto us—but Jesus extends the notion of neighbor beyond imagination. Our neighbor includes the hungry, the naked, and the imprisoned, and Jesus invites us to feed, clothe, and visit them in jail. Our neighbor includes the rejected, the demonized, and the outcast, and Jesus asks us to invite them to our table. Our neighbor includes those who have wounded us, even unceasingly, and Jesus admonishes us to forgive them, just as we have been forgiven. Our neighbor includes those who actively violate us, and Jesus emboldens us to turn the other cheek and go the extra mile. Our neighbor even includes those with whom we are mired in violent and oppressive conflict, and these are the people to whom

Jesus refers when he urges us to love our enemies, to bless those who curse us, to pray for those who persecute us, and to show compassion to those who hate and do evil. (See Matthew 5:44; Luke 6:27-28.)

This radical ethic of compassion seems extraordinary to the point of being unattainable—or attainable only to the gifted few. When an Amish community finds the capacity to forgive a man who killed its schoolchildren, when Nelson Mandela finds it in his heart to invite his jailer of twenty-seven years to stand at his side during his inauguration, when a Palestinian woman who has lost her son in a terrorist bombing raises an Israeli boy as a Jew, these actions shimmer with the miraculous. Ordinary folk like us often feel indicted or shamed that our own unhealed grief or rage or fear still grips us with such force that we cannot conceive of such compassion, let alone want to cultivate it. Or out of a sense of Christian obligation, we suppress our feelings toward our adversaries and feign a forced civility that only masks our darker emotions seething below the surface. Sometimes this takes the form of denying our power altogether and simply submitting passively to indignity, which only leaves the violation unchecked and our own indignation to fester. To be sure, shame, suppression, and passive submission are poisonous to our spiritual lives; they may be well-intentioned, but they are missteps on the spiritual path that Jesus teaches.

For Jesus, compassion inspires a genuine loving regard that flows freely from the heart. It is rooted in the restorative compassion of God that is given to all humanity. The radicality of his path is that the healing power of sacred compassion holds us precisely where we are—in our fears and angers, our shames and suppressions, even in our resistance to wanting to love at all. Indeed, within these shadowy impulses we can experience more deeply the healing and renewing presence of God and become filled with a compassion that extends not only toward these very reactivities raging within us but also toward those who trigger them in the first place. Jesus offers a thoroughly sincere invitation. Not only can we learn to love our neighbors as ourselves, but also we can learn to love our enemies, even as God so loves us all.

A Threefold Heartbeat of Transformative Compassion

Jesus' spiritual path of radical compassion has three dimensions: a deepening of our connection to the compassion of God, a restoration to a humanity fully loved and alive, and an increase to our capacity to be instruments of compassion toward others in the world. These three movements flow from the heartbeat of God. Hearts pulsate in an ever-renewing, threefold rhythm. They gather weary and broken blood cells into their center, they replenish and restore them into health and vitality, and they pump the cells back into the body to heal wounds and replenish tissue. As the cells become depleted, the heart's rhythm continues—drawing those cells once more into its center, restoring and replenishing them, and pumping them back into the body. Similarly, God's heart beats in an ever-flowing, threefold pulse. God dwells at the center of creation—in the center of our being—as a source of life and love, inviting broken humanity to rest in the healing bosom of compassion, to be restored into a humanity loved and alive, and to pulsate into our wounded world as agents of compassion. We complete this cycle only to return again to the source of God's love, become replenished, and enter once again into the body of our broken world.[8]

Jesus' spiritual path invites us to participate ever more fully in the three movements of this sacred rhythm. Through this process, the pulse of our lives beats more in harmony with the pulse of God flowing through creation. The process transforms the very rhythms of our hearts to beat as one with God's heart that aches for the world. In the ancient world, people spoke of the heart as the vital center of the body. Our heart's focus determines our deepest allegiances, investments, passions, and pursuits. As Jesus observes, "For where your treasure is, there your heart will be also" (Luke 12:34). Jesus cautions against centering our hearts on such anemic spiritual fare as wealth, honor, and social positioning. Instead, our heart is most healthy and vital when centered on God. Yet we do not measure a heart centered on God by external religious piety—keeping the commandments, partaking in rituals, paying tithes, and the like. Piety, though cultically exacting and morally blameless, can still flow from an impure heart when harboring, for example, self-righteousness or a disdain for the religiously inferior.

For Jesus, the essence of a pure heart is its compassion. A heart becomes pure when it is rooted in the heart of God, the cosmic heart in which we live and move and have our being. Indeed, a pure heart soaks up the compassion of God, beats in sync with God's own pulse, and bears more fully God's heart for the world. A heart that beats at one with God's is a heart that holds others with care, savors and celebrates their healing and vitality, and supports them as they move through the world in pursuit of life and love. This heart grows increasingly more tender and beats with the pulse of compassion.

A Garden of Compassion

James Worthington has seen firsthand a heart that beats to the pulse of compassion. James runs an inner-city youth program that offers young people an alternative to the deceptive lures of gang life. He tells his kids about Raul Torres, a former custodian in their own community. Raul lived with his wife of forty-five years on a modest corner lot in South Central Los Angeles. When his wife died of a stroke in her sleep, Raul was grief-stricken. He retired from his job, sought solace from his church, and spent long hours staring at the yard from the porch his wife adored.

Raul decided to plant a memorial garden for his wife. It spanned the entire corner lot and contained flower beds, boxes of herbs and vegetables, tomatoes on the vine, cilantro in bundles, and rows of his beloved's favorite—prize-worthy roses of a dozen different hues. For Raul, the garden served as both a tender tribute and a second life in his later years.

One morning, Raul discovered that several rosebushes had been demolished. Shreds of blossom and bush were strewn on the ground as if they had been assaulted with a baseball bat. He was certain who had done it—a carload of local gang members had taken to cruising the neighborhood, driving by slowly and casing it with their cold, vacant stares.

Afraid of doing anything else, Raul simply swept up the mess, repaired the bushes, and tended the garden as if nothing had happened. Two days later, another bush was attacked. A few days later, yet another one. Angry and afraid, heartsick and powerless, Raul was beside himself about what to do. On the off chance it would deter the vandals, he sat in stoic vigil at the living room window.

That is when Raul saw the boy. He vaguely knew his story. The ten-year-old lived alone with his mother. His father had been gone for years, and his brother, a gang member, was in jail for killing a rival. In retaliation for the murder his brother committed, a drive-by occurred at the boy's home. His leg was nicked by a bullet. Though scarcely limping any longer, the boy still walked with a cane. Raul watched him, presumably on his way to school. When he got to the roses, the boy wielded the cane like a weapon and lashed out at one of the bushes. Once done with the attack, he started to leave but then stopped. He noticed Raul staring from the window. The boy looked scared, as if caught with nowhere to go. Then he glared in defiance and swiftly scrambled away.

Raul's first instinct was to chase the boy down and scold him. His second was to call the police and turn in the truant. But he could not shake the look in the boy's eyes. It was as if Raul could see it all—the boy's loneliness, the rage, the terror, the futility, and lacing throughout, the despair that would make a future in gang life all but inevitable. Raul did not have the heart to call the police. He let the boy's eyes haunt him until he had an idea.

That afternoon, Raul found the boy walking home from school and approached him. The boy hardened in defiance. Raul told him that he was having trouble with his garden—someone was destroying his flowers. The boy insisted it wasn't him, that he didn't know a thing about it. That wasn't what he meant, Raul assured him. He needed someone to help him protect the flowers and to help him care for them from time to time. He'd pay him, let him plant his own bushes, and teach him how to grow plants if the boy wanted. The boy was skeptical. Raul offered that they try it for one week. The boy just had to keep an eye on the garden, and on Saturday morning he would get paid.

On Saturday, the boy showed up. He stayed the better part of the day. Raul taught him how to tend the roses and helped him plant a rosebush of his own. They harvested tomatoes and cut fresh herbs. At day's end, they picked a bag full of lemons and made fresh lemonade. It was the best the boy had ever tasted. It was so good, the boy came back the following week and the next.

To this day, James asserts, the garden has never been vandalized again. He would know—he's the boy who bludgeoned the roses. And this neighborhood is still his turf. He works there with other young people, offering them a place to flourish in the midst of the ever-present violence.

Raul Torres's heart beats to the pulse of compassion. The spiritual path he exemplifies is threefold. First, the path deepens his connection to God's compassion. Raul roots himself in God's extravagant love. He senses this love throughout his world—in a spouse's care, in the gifts of the earth, in an evening's quiet, and in weekly worship. At such times, he brushes close to and is renewed by a cosmic presence of compassion so empathic that it holds with healing care his deepest wounds and secret shames and so expansive that it holds and heals the blood-soaked suffering even of those enraged enough to be violent. Raul's capacity for care, healing, and vitality flows from the compassion of the God he knows.

Second, Raul's path liberates him from the internal turbulence that can disconnect him from his compassionate core. Through most of our waking hours, emotions of fear, anger, anxiety, and stress assail us. Impulses— for example, to work, run errands, do chores, and numb out—drive us. Internal monologues of self-critique, perfectionism, blame, and judgment hound us. All of this alienates us from the loving people we know ourselves to be. We seldom feel at the tiller of our lives; instead, the winds of the moment hurl us about, and we swallow water from the waves of passions and voices from within.

As Raul Torres reveals to us, even within the riptides of grief, despair, fear, and indignation, we can find freedom from the tumult of our inner world. We can cultivate a grounded internal stability that quiets the cacophony, anchors our power, and restores our capacity for purposeful action. The power that stills these storms within us is compassion turned inward. Self-compassion provides the secret to interior freedom and personal restoration. The raging heart of a ten-year-old delinquent relaxes before the face of care and understanding. So too does the raging heart within us. When we extend to ourselves the understanding and care we would to a suffering child, the tempest within subsides, solid ground appears, and the way forward reveals itself to us. Self-compassion brings us home to ourselves.

Third, Raul's spiritual path increases his capacity to be an instrument of compassion toward others in the world. Raul's compassion sees others free from the distortions of his own fears and wounds. It recognizes the inherent dignity and unique beauty within each person, even those most damaged; is moved by another's suffering, however well hidden; and extends a word or gesture of kindness that might ease pain, deepen joy, or foster a restoration of beaten-down humanity. Such connection and care can be cultivated toward colleagues in the workplace, loved ones at home, and the person next door or at the supermarket. In such moments, our heart flows freely with the pulse of compassion. We feel human. We feel like ourselves.

Yet the reach of compassion extends radically further. As Raul Torres shows us, we can cultivate compassion not only toward our friends, allies, and associates but also toward our opponents, our enemies, people who trigger us, and people who accost us. In our fight or flight world, our only two options in the face of aggression appear to be passivity or retaliation. Whether in reaction to a loved one who yells at us, a coworker mistreating us, an adversary demeaning us, or an assailant violating the work of our hands, our response to assault defaults into submissive endurance or counterattack.

The path of compassion points to another way. To be sure, this way stands up to violation—protects the vulnerable, empowers the victimized, holds offenders accountable, and restrains the unrepentant. However, it does so in ways that refuse to demonize the other, even those whose deeds are monstrous; in ways that recognize the suffering of the attacker, even underneath his or her attempts to inflict pain; and in ways that invite the offender's restoration to the community on the condition that he or she makes amends and acts humanely. We can meet adversaries with empowered constraint, empathic understanding, and a genuine sense of restorative care. When we do, we retain our own humanity.

A transformed heart beats to the pulse of compassion. Its rhythms bear the rhythms of God's heartbeat for the world. Its pulse resuscitates our own spirit. Its pulse revives the spirit of another deadened into brutality. Compassion bears the sacred breath of life.

Yet, truth be told, cultivating compassion can be difficult.

The Problem Is *How*

So how do we actually cultivate compassion? How do we harmonize our heartbeats to the pulse of compassion? Within the cacophony of violence that rips apart the world around and within us, Jesus is tuned into a sacred song that restores the compassionate core of humanity. But the madness that mires us can be relentless. How, precisely, do we hear this music and move to its life-giving rhythms?

How do we know this compassionate God in our bones when the secret shames that infest our soul breed the terror that God is cold and disgusted? How do we find the interior freedom that stills the noise of our inner lives and begets authentic self-compassion?

And in a world where violence stalks our streets, schools, churches, and families, how do we truly love our enemies? Enemies are the people we detest and demonize. They threaten us, they are dangerous, and they stand against all we hold sacred. Whether a bully with a platform, a thug with a weapon, or a bigot who pushes our buttons, an enemy incites rage, repulsion, and an instinct to attack or run for cover. How do we love our enemy—a stepfather who abused us, for example—when his impassive unrepentance incenses us? How do we love our enemy when, driven by perfectionism and our own castigation, our enemy is ourselves? How do we love our enemy when our enemy, the person who most repels and infuriates us, is our very own child, partner, or parent? And what if the person still poses a threat? How can we have compassion and still protect the vulnerable, empower the victimized, and hold a perpetrator appropriately accountable?

The way of radical compassion can prove challenging and complex. Its music can seem dim, its dance steps obscure. And yet, its song leads to life. It leads us back to our humanity.

This book shows how. This book provides a primer on Christian compassion. If Jesus were to create a school of compassion, this book could serve as an introductory text. It summarizes his vision of the threefold nature of compassion. Moreover, it describes the spiritual and social practices by which we actually become more compassionate—in relation to God, toward ourselves, and toward the people in our lives. While many extol the importance of compassion, this book practically describes how to cultivate it in our lives.

To be sure, the way is radical. It journeys through the most unlikely of places. It faces with grounded boldness both the madness that sabotages our souls from within and that which ravages our world from without. And in the muck of that madness, it stands with Jesus listening for a song. The song flows from the heartbeat of God. And it invites creation to move to its rhythms. The spiritual path of Jesus choreographs those rhythms. It offers patterns of steps that bear a specific promise. As we soak in the healing sound of this music and sway to these restorative movements, we will find ourselves dancing to the song of creation and moving in time with the Divine—that sacred heartbeat that not only takes away the mad in our world but also transforms that mad into the compassion that children and saints know so well.

Chapter 1

The Pulse of Compassion

The Core Practice That Sustains the Way

In January of 1995, Azim Khamisa awakened to find a business card tucked in his door from the homicide division of the San Diego police department. Azim called the number on the card, and an officer shared with him the tragedy. Azim's only son, a twenty-year-old college student named Tariq, was delivering a pizza during the night in a neighborhood known for occasional gang violence. As Tariq sat in his car, another car pinned him from behind. Two teens got out. Tony Hicks, all of fourteen years old, was handed a gun by an older teen, the gang leader. Tony was ordered to take down the unknown deliveryman. Tony obeyed. He shot Tariq one time, the bullet piercing Tariq's heart. Within several minutes, Tariq suffocated in his own blood. The officer had come to inform Azim that his son was found dead at the scene.

In the months that followed, Azim struggled with rage, helplessness, despair, even thoughts of vengeance. A devout Muslim, he also struggled with the Islamic invitation to resist being consumed by hatred and to find a way to forgive even the unforgivable. He took care not to act out in his anger, but he didn't suppress it. He meditated prayerfully and sought therapy for his grief. Over time, the pain subsided, and Azim felt a sacred presence sustaining him. That sacred presence was expansive. It held him and his family. It held his slain son, Tariq. And it also held the boy so troubled that violence toward a stranger felt attractive.

Azim came to realize that there were victims on both sides of the gun. Not only was his son killed but also an African American fourteen-year-old boy—raised fatherless in poverty and ubiquitous racism—was tried as an adult and then tossed away into a prison cell for the unforeseeable future. Azim decided that the cycle of despair and violence must come to an end. He quit his job and created a foundation, named after his son, dedicated to eradicating the conditions of youth violence and teaching young people a peacemaker's path of nonviolence, forgiveness, and restorative justice. He invited the teenaged killer's grandfather to join him. Then Azim visited Tony in prison.

Though Azim had already felt some forgiveness in his heart, he grew anxious as he waited in the jail's grated visiting booth. He was unsure what he would feel when his son's slayer sat across from him. He imagined looking into the gang member's eyes and seeing the face of a cold-blooded killer. He prayed for mercy. Tony entered the visiting booth, and Azim looked into his eyes. He did not see a killer. He saw a terrified child, beaten down by a world stacked against him.

As Azim described it, he gazed straight into Tony's soul and saw the boy's humanity. In that moment of connection, both of their hearts broke open, and both hearts were touched by a sacred grace. Azim shared—without malice or accusation—the grief of losing a son. And he listened to Tony share the pain of growing up fatherless in a gang-ridden ghetto. He wept for Tony. Tony wept as well, expressing how sorry he was and how he ached for some way to make it up. Azim offered Tony a way. Indeed, he did more; he offered Tony a job. Upon his release from prison, Tony could work as an advocate against youth violence through the foundation named after the very boy Tony had killed.[1]

The Essential Components of Compassion

Jesus' spiritual path, at its essence, entails the cultivation of compassion. It invites us to become ever more grounded in God's expansive compassion, ever more restored in a self-compassion that tames our chaotic interior lives, and ever more fully an agent of care, a beacon of compassion within our bruised and battered world. To embark upon this spiritual path, we first must understand what compassion is. Azim Khamisa—in a rather radical way—embodies compassion. Though often less dramatic, we all can recognize compassionate actions: a mother sees her child ravaged by fever and cradles the loved one in her soothing arms, a colleague loses her job and a coworker offers support, an earthquake or tsunami devastates a country and people from around the world provide relief. However faintly, the pulse of compassion beats within us all.

The essence of this pulse is straightforward. We define compassion as simply being moved in our depths by others' experiences and responding in a way that intends either to ease their suffering or promote their flourishing. As the word is used in the Gospels, compassion is what Jesus feels and how he responds to the blind (see Matthew 20:34), the hungry (see Matthew 15:32; Mark 8:2), and the widow who loses her only son (see Luke 7:13). The waiting father feels compassion for his wandering prodigal, and he runs to embrace his son and welcome him home. (See Luke 15:20.) The good Samaritan feels compassion for the man beaten on the side of the road, and he offers him healing care. (See Luke 10:33.)

Metaphorically, compassion is a movement of the heart, the quiver we feel, for example, when we see someone in pain.[2] The compassionate heart, we say, is soft and tender. In contrast to the cold or hard heart of someone unmoved by suffering, a compassionate heart beats freely, supple enough to take in another's pain, be moved, and respond with acts of kindness, goodwill, healing, and justice. Azim Khamisa provides an example. Softened by grief and broken by suffering, his heart is neither numb to the presence of his son's killer before him nor hardened with feelings of vengeance and bitterness. Rather, it is softened such that it takes in Tony's tragic reality; is moved to tender understanding and care; then responds with forgiveness, an invitation to make amends, and the promise of a future awaiting his release. Azim's heart beats to the pulse of compassion.

Often this pulse occurs naturally and with an elegant simplicity, like when a child notices a wounded puppy, is moved by its mournful eyes, and soothes it with a tender caress. Other times, like with Azim Khamisa, the process is agonizing and complex, requiring a sustained commitment to healing and the spiritual practices that support it. Either way, this compassionate pulse, when examined more closely, contains several essential components. While sometimes implicit—or so subtle as to seem instinctive—every experience of compassion involves the following six dimensions:

1. *Paying attention* (Contemplative awareness). A precondition for compassion is a particular way of seeing others. Usually when we relate to one another we do so through judgments and reactions that are conditioned by our own needs, desires, feelings, and sensitivities. We

do not see other persons on their own terms; rather, we perceive them through the filtered lenses of our own agendas. I seldom see my son, Justin, for example, in the poignant particularity of his longings, fears, wounds, and delights. I usually see him as the forgetful college kid who neglects to pick up his dishes or the straight-A student about whom I like to brag to my colleagues. Either way, he becomes objectified through my own personal agenda, not a subject with depth and uniqueness.

Contemplative awareness, as Walter J. Burghardt classically defined it, entails "a long, loving look at the real."[3] We experience contemplative awareness through the nonreactive, nonprojective apprehension of others in the mystery of their uniqueness. Azim sees contemplatively not when Tony is demonized as a cold-blooded killer or even lauded as the trophy of a restorative justice program but when Azim pays attention to Tony, peers into his very soul, and glimpses the terrified boy in lockdown orange who longs for restoration. The recipient of our gaze knows the difference between being seen and being objectified. Compassion engenders the sense of truly being seen without the distortional filter of another's judgments or agenda.

2. *Understanding empathically* (Empathic care). Compassion entails being moved by another's experience. In Hebrew (*rachum*) and Greek (*splanchnizomai*), the etymological roots for the primary words translated as *compassion* are linked to a person's vital organs—specifically the womb, heart, belly, and bowels.[4] In essence, when we are moved to compassion, our depths are stirred—often viscerally. When God gazes upon the Israelites enslaved and oppressed in Egypt or when Jesus sees the woman beside her son's dead body, they are gut-wrenched before the suffering, heartbroken, sickened to the stomach, their womb-like core contracts. In contrast to the coldness and indifference of the unmoved, a compassionate person allows another's pain or joy to reverberate within his or her deepest core such that he or she is moved to pathos before the other's suffering or stirred to delight before the other's flourishing. A compassionate person understands, in his or her depths, the wounds, heartaches, and longings at the core of another person's behavior and experience.

Azim understands Tony's experience. When he sees into the soul of the boy who killed his son, Azim is moved by Tony's pain and understands the wounds and oppressions that gave rise to Tony's behavior. Again, the recipient knows the difference between someone who cares about his or her personal experience and someone who is inattentive or simply uncaring. In the language of attachment theory, the recipient feels as if someone gets what he or she feels to the point of full understanding.[5]

3. *Loving with connection* (All-accepting presence). A nonjudgmental, all-embracing, infinitely loving quality of presence resides at the core of compassion. Like a mother cradling her child, the love of compassion carries no hint of shame, critique, aversion, or belittlement. Rather, it wells up with a connective care that extends toward others like the soothing wash of the sunlight's warmth.

   Jesus gazes at the gathered crowd aching for a leader, and his heart fills with the loving regard of a shepherd eager to care for his flock. As Azim sees and is moved by the broken boy before him, love expands within him and flows out of him, connecting him to Tony, even through the bulletproof glass of a prison visiting room. In turn, when softened to receive it, Tony feels accepted, forgiven, and known. Azim's presence enables Tony to grieve in the face of the pain he has caused and ache to be restored to his own humanity.

4. *Sensing the sacredness* (Spiritual expansiveness). Compassion is a spiritual energy. When our hearts open to others' suffering and a sustaining love flows through us, the veil of the everyday world we live in is pierced and relativized: time seems to stop, errands lose their urgency, perennial irritations feel petty and frivolous. In those moments, our spirits expand— our capacity to care deepens, our understanding for the plight of others extends, and our patience seems infinite. Grace abounds.

   Some people experience these compassion-filled moments as holy. These moments serve as icons of a sacred energy, cosmic and benevolent. They are portals of presence that remind us that compassion flows not only from our hearts but also from the very texture of the universe. We are plugged into and instruments of the Holy Spirit, whose loving energy reverberates throughout all time and space, holds with care every scar and wound no matter how deep or brutal, and seeps through the open heart willing to be the instrument through which it might soothe another.

   Jesus embodies compassion and incarnates the very presence of God. Bearing the same spirit, Azim sees into Tony's soul, and a whispered hush descends upon them both. Ordinary time becomes sacred. Azim experiences his own spirit as expanded, a fuller and freer channel of God's love in which he too is held and healed. And Tony glimpses not only that this large-hearted man is holding him with healing care but also that this man's heart beats with the sacred love of the universe that holds and heals as well. For a moment, Azim and Tony are held together by the divine presence that sustains them both. The cosmic sea of God's love has found a channel through which to pour itself into the arid soil of a maximum security prison. And in those sacred waters, all wounds are healed.

5. *Embodying new life* (Desire for flourishing). Compassion not only grieves with the wounded in pain but also yearns for the transformation of suffering into joy. Compassion celebrates when new life is birthed and embodied. Like the womb that receives and incubates with protective care, holding others' pain brings about life. Genuine compassion is not limited to moments of suffering, offering an empathic connection only as long as others are in pain. Genuine compassion takes as much delight in others' flourishing as it feels pathos for their pain. Indeed, pathos, when soaked with compassionate care, gives rise to the yearning that wounded persons flourish with abundant life.

Jesus is filled with joy at the widow's ecstatic relief as she clasps her risen son. The prodigal's father throws a party and adorns his son in rings and a robe. Likewise, Azim feels sorrow in the face of Tony's suffering, but that sorrow swells into the aching desire for Tony to know healing and step into wholeness. And should the day come when Tony walks free from prison, a compassionate Azim will be the first to greet him and celebrate Tony's rehabilitation. Compassion's tears sometimes come from joy, and they flow freely when lives are healed.

6. *Act* (Restorative action). The sentiment of compassion does not close in on itself. It does not soak in a moment of tender pathos and then simply walk away. Compassion responds. It takes some step toward easing others' suffering and nurturing their flourishing. A mother cradling a sick child searches for medicine that will heal, images of a hurricane's destruction give rise to relief trips delivering supplies and repairing the damage, and Azim sees an imprisoned boy and is moved to participate in the boy's rehabilitation.

Compassion includes restorative action. Without it, compassion degenerates into sentimentality—feeling bad for others' pain but ultimately abandoning them to fend for themselves. Compassion walks toward, not away. It sits with the grieving, companions the forlorn, and walks shoulder to shoulder with those on the road pushing toward liberation. As the Jewish rabbi Abraham Heschel remembered about his time with Martin Luther King Jr. at the Selma march in 1965, in the work of compassion, there comes a time when we must pray with our legs.

These six dimensions compose the essential PULSE of compassion. In short, we define compassion as:

P—*Paying attention.* Perceiving another's experience with a nonjudgmental, nonreactive clarity.

U—*Understanding empathically.* Being moved by the sometimes hidden suffering within that person.

L—*Loving with connection.* Being filled with and extending an all-embracing care.

S—*Sensing the sacredness.* Recognizing and savoring the sacred source of compassion that holds and heals all wounds.

E—*Embodying new life.* Yearning for the restorative flourishing to be birthed within another.

ACT—Then, from the PULSE of this compassionate connection, we respond with tangible acts of healing, kindness, and care.

Both Jesus and Azim Khamisa exemplified these characteristics. Their heart beats to the pulse of compassion. When they perceive tragically broken persons, Jesus and Azim are moved by their pain—so moved that they offer their own hands in transforming that pain into redemption.

Distilling the Way of Radical Compassion

Jesus offers a spiritual path that cultivates such compassion. Many times compassion comes easily and naturally, like a child seeing a wounded bird and spontaneously tending to its broken wing. When whole and vital, our hearts automatically beat with care and connection. Often, however, much less sympathetic impulses drive our lives. The pulse of our spirit accelerates with drivenness or hyper-reactivity, it shuts down and dulls with numbness or fatigue, and it beats erratically in cycles of rage and withdrawal or compulsion and shame. Sometimes, compassion requires cultivation—the pulse of our lives feels off, it beats out of sync with the pulse of God's love, and it requires restoration to the tender heartbeat of care.

At such times, the spiritual path of Jesus offers us a way to realign ourselves with God, to restore the pulse of our spirit, and to resuscitate and sustain our God-given capacities to embody care in the world. This spiritual path contains four rhythmic movements that transform the depleted or hardened heart to beat once more in harmony with the loving heartbeat of God. This fourfold rhythm entails deepening our connection with the expansive compassion of God, cultivating a self-compassion that recalibrates our erratic pulse to the steady pulse of our restored humanity, cultivating a compassion for the suffering that afflicts someone's humanity, and responding with concrete acts of embodied care and connection.

This fourfold rhythm is coordinated in the Compassion Practice, a practical way of embodying the way of Jesus within the messiness of our lives. It is designed for those times when the pulse of our lives beats out of sync with the sacred pulse of compassion. When our hearts feel hard, cold, reactive, or depleted—when a shopper, for example, dominates the express lane with a basketful of groceries, we may burn with impatience and indignation; when a loved one needs a shoulder to cry on, we may sigh with burden and fatigue; or when a tragedy strikes our family, we may find ourselves mired in a pit of outrage and pain—the Compassion Practice, which synthesizes the spiritual path of Jesus, offers a path toward restoration. When we feel disconnected from the compassionate people we yearn to be—from the compassionate people God created us to be—the Compassion Practice invites us to

1. ***Catch your breath*** (Get grounded). Our native wisdom is revealing. Whenever someone feels agitated, we instinctively say, "Take a deep breath." Likewise, when we are swept up in a current of emotions, passions, impulses, and drives that distort our capacities to care, our first

move is to find solid ground. Acting out at the mercy of the drives and passions of our inner world only wreaks havoc for others and for us. We need to secure some distance—emotionally and, if necessary, physically—that allows our emotions to settle. Taking a time-out, walking outdoors, going on a retreat, finding a moment to ourselves or with God, or simply catching our breath solidifies our footing until the ground feels safe or sacred enough to engage the situation more clearly. This "moment" may need to last for a season. As would any of us, Azim Khamisa required ample space for healing before compassionate forgiveness could seem anything but offensive.

Catching our breath also entails returning to the source of life and love that renews and sustains us. The springs of compassion flow from the sacred pools of God's love that sustain all creation. We can only give of that which we have received. When we feel depleted or disconnected, God invites us to return to the well and to drink deeply once more from the restorative waters of sacred compassion. In doing so, we remember the truth of who we are—beloved in our core—and how we are sustained by God's breath of life and renewal.

2. *Take your PULSE* (Cultivate compassion for yourself). When we feel disconnected from our compassionate nature, our pulse beats erratically—gripped perhaps by repulsion, fear, or envy—or grows dim with numbness and fatigue. The invitation, once grounded, is to take a U-turn, to look inward, and to recalibrate our pulse to the steady heartbeat of humanity.[6]

When we feel agitated, reactive, or depleted, our inner world is in pain and in need. Ignoring the state of our soul and pressing to cultivate compassion for another is not only counterproductive but also a form of interior violence. It dismisses the needs and suffering that cry out from within us. Forcing an open heart toward others while closing our own heart to ourselves is as internally contradictory as screaming our way into silence, straining our way into relaxation, or battling our way into inner peace. The cry within us will only intensify and demand our attention in other ways, such as compassion fatigue, an intractable resentment, or a chronic knot in our neck. In the early days of his grief, Azim wisely heeded the impulse that he could not yet face his son's killer. He needed to turn inward; he had healing to do and personal power to restore.

Self-compassion restores us to the steady heartbeat of our humanity. As we turn inward, we extend to ourselves the same compassion we would extend to others. Following the essential components of compassion, this essentially entails taking our own PULSE.

P—*Paying attention.* Cultivate a nonjudgmental, nonreactive awareness of whatever agitation is present within you.

U—*Understanding empathically.* Listen for and be moved by the suffering hidden within the cry of this agitation—the fear, longing, or aching wound in need of tending.

L—*Loving with connection.* As you are moved by the suffering within you, extend tender care toward the need or wound that presents itself.

S—*Sensing the sacredness.* Recognize and savor the infinite expanse of God's compassion that holds and heals the suffering within you.

E—*Embodying new life.* Notice the gifts and qualities of restored humanity that are being birthed within you.

In taking our PULSE, we not only relax the reactivities, repulsions, fears, and drives that distort our natural humanity but also tend to the wounds and needs hidden within them. In so doing, we are restored to our naturally compassionate selves.

3. *Take the other's PULSE* (Cultivate compassion for another). Once our hearts are steady enough to be open to empathic connection with others—this may take time and many U-turns—we can cultivate genuine compassion for others. We do so, as we did with ourselves, by connecting with the PULSE of humanity beating within them.

P—*Paying attention.* Cultivate a nonjudgmental, nonreactive awareness of what the person is doing and how he or she is doing it.

U—*Understanding empathically.* Listen for and be moved by the suffering hidden within the cry of his or her emotions or behavior—the fear, longing, or aching wound in need of care.

L—*Loving with connection.* As the suffering within the other person moves you, extend care toward the need or wound that surfaces.

S—*Sensing the sacredness.* Recognize and savor the infinite expanse of God's compassion that holds and heals his or her wounds.

E—*Embodying new life.* Notice the gifts and qualities of restored humanity that are being birthed within the person and yearn for his or her flourishing.

This pulse of humanity beats, however dimly, within all of us. No matter how distorted and beaten down we may become, an abiding capacity for care and connection remains alive within us. Azim discovered this pulse in a hardened boy who killed at age fourteen. Many of the persons we encounter routinely, however, have not had their humanity all but obliterated. The people we more commonly engage are like us—momentarily mired in the compulsions, fears, and sensitivities of surviving everyday life. Nevertheless, as long as our hearts are beating, the pulse of our humanity lives. Connecting with this pulse within others unlocks our genuine compassion, and such compassion has the power to soften even the most hardened of hearts.

4. *Decide what to do* (Discern compassionate action). As previously mentioned, compassion includes restorative action. We have not cultivated compassion when we simply experience feelings of warm

regard toward ourselves or others. We must act out our compassion in ways that ease suffering and promote the flourishing of others. Such acts include consoling the grief-stricken, tending the wounded, and befriending those who feel forsaken. But acting out of genuine compassion often requires careful discernment. What does compassion look like, for example, when the wound caused by another is still fresh or when an offender refuses to curb his or her violence and remains unrepentant?

Compassionate action must serve and sustain our own healing and restoration. The act of cultivating compassion does not invite us to minimize our needs for healing and wholeness, silence our voices, abandon our personal power, or lose ourselves in endless caretaking to the point of depletion and fatigue. Compassion yearns for the flourishing of *all* life, including our own. Our capacity for genuine compassion flows out of the strength and fullness of our vitality. Whenever we are disconnected from our capacities for compassion, our own wounds remain in need of attention.

Compassionate action also invites the restoration of others. In the case of an offense against us, such restoration demands accountability. Compassion is not sentimental. Violent actions create wounds, and perpetrators must be held responsible. Azim had compassion for Tony and then offered him a chance to heal and rehabilitate. Their relationship was restored only because Tony was willing to take responsibility for his actions, show remorse, commit to his own recovery, and, to the best of his ability, make amends by devoting his life to the prevention of further teenaged violence. Azim's compassion paved the way, but the restoration of Tony's humanity and the possibility of reconciliation required Tony to walk the road.

And what if Tony had refused, turned defiant, or remained unrepentant? Azim's compassion could still hold strong in the midst of the horrors perpetrated by Tony and Tony's defiance. However, Azim's compassion would carry a resolve: A dangerous man should be sequestered, and his unchecked violence must be prevented from affecting other families. Compassion does not endorse the perpetuation of violation. But it does seek the ember of humanity in even the most violent of offenders. With grief for tragedy and an assertive determination to safeguard life, compassion limits violence even as it appeals to the perpetrator's humanity.

These essential movements—the core rhythms that restore us to our compassionate essence—make up the Compassion Practice, illustrated in the graphic on the following page. Layers of intricacy are yet to be detailed, as are various capacities that enhance the process's effectiveness. But for all the complexities hidden within, the fundamental movement of compassion remains elegantly simple. Whenever we feel disconnected from our compassionate core, we can follow this pattern: *Catch your breath. Take your PULSE. Take the other's PULSE.* Then, and only then, *decide what to do and do it.* In regulating the pulse of our humanity and deepening our connection with the pulse of another, compassion flows through us—a compassion that pulsates from the heartbeat of divine love that holds and sustains the whole universe.

Coda

To this day, Azim Khamisa works with young people in communities ravaged by gang violence. He also works tirelessly for Tony Hicks's release from prison. Tony has earned advanced degrees, written hundreds of letters to marginalized youth much like him, and tirelessly advocated for alternatives to violence. Together, Azim and Tony bear testimony that compassion is possible even in the most tragic of circumstances. In situations where victims lie on both sides of a gun, Azim and Tony point to the hope and possibility of healing. The compassion they embody is not limited to saints and exemplars but is available to us all. Jesus teaches us how. He leads us to the extravagant love that restores the heartbeat of our humanity.

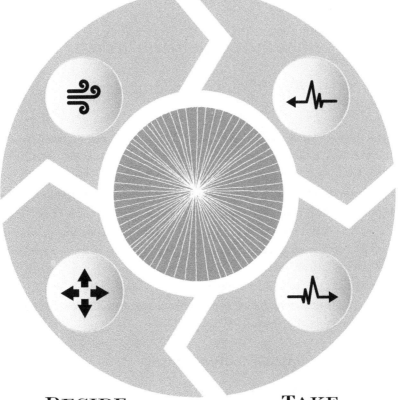

CATCH YOUR BREATH

Get grounded.

TAKE YOUR PULSE

Cultivate compassion for yourself.

DECIDE WHAT TO DO

Discern compassionate action.

TAKE THE OTHER'S PULSE

Cultivate compassion for another.

Chapter 2

Catching Our Breath

Grounding Ourselves in the

Divine Source of Compassion

For Jesus, compassion begins with God. The God he knows, teaches, and incarnates is a God of extravagant and unequivocal compassion. God is the source from which compassion flows; God's compassionate Spirit sustains all life. The first step in cultivating compassion is to remember, rest in, and be renewed by this grounding sacred presence. Jesus invites us to know God's compassion in every fiber of our being, to experience ourselves as beloved in every part of who we are, and to be as fused with God's sustaining presence as with the steady flow of breath that sustains our bodies. When we feel disconnected from this compassionate flow, when our souls gasp for the air that restores, our spiritual invitation is to catch our breath and become grounded in the sacred love that holds and heals all things.

Grounded Compassion in Birmingham

In 1962, Rev. Dr. Martin Luther King Jr. attended a weeklong Christian leadership conference in Birmingham, Alabama. At the time, Birmingham was the most thoroughly segregated city in America. Schools, swimming pools, public parks and bathrooms, drinking fountains, fitting rooms, and even checkout stands in grocery stores were designated with the placards reading *Colored* or *Whites Only*. Indeed, the crusade to preserve segregation was so extreme that a children's book was banned in the libraries, stores, and public schools for showing black and white sheep together on the same cover.

Tensions were high. Thaddeus Eugene "Bull" Connor, the Commissioner of Public Safety, dispersed a rally of schoolchildren by knocking them off their feet with fire hoses and then unleashing his attack dogs on them. African Americans were routinely raped, lynched, castrated, and spat upon. Churches were vandalized. Civic leaders were beaten. The neighborhood where black activists lived was bombed so many times that the newspapers dubbed it "Dynamite Hill."

Into this war zone of racial tension King came to preach his gospel of love and to encourage the people to begin nonviolent campaigns of boycotting stores, staging sit-ins at restaurants, and marching through the streets in peaceful protest against the indignities of segregation and racism.

During his visit, King addressed a crowd of people at a church. The place was packed. People filled the pews and the aisles, the window alcoves and balconies. Even the parking lot was fitted with speakers for the overflowing crowd. As King began his closing remarks, a white man stood up and walked toward him. King was weary. His house had been bombed three times already. He had received death threats in the mail for years. He had been stabbed in the chest while delivering a sermon in Harlem. But not until the man was directly in front of him did King see the hatred in the man's eyes. The man lunged at King, knocked him backward, and beat him on the face and back. The church erupted. A mob swarmed around King, grabbed the attacker, and herded him toward the door. Cries rang out, "Kill the bastard! Lynch him! Beat him to a bloody pulp!" And into the midst of all the cacophonous chaos, one voice boomed through the room: "Stop! Leave him alone."

The church fell silent. The voice they heard was Martin Luther King Jr.'s, his face transcendently calm. King walked over to the man, put his arm around the assailant's shoulder, and looked around the crowd.

"What would you like to do?" King asked the crowd. "Kill him? That isn't our movement. Would you like to use Molotov cocktails? That is not our movement. I'll tell you what our movement is. It's to understand him. Yes, even him. It's to ask what it would be like if you were taught since you were a child, since you were baby enough to crawl, that the Negro is a *thing*! If you were taught from your parents, from your teachers, from even your ministers and the people sitting next to you in church that it isn't wrong to hate, what would you be then? That's what this movement is. It's to reveal these people to themselves."[1]

Martin Luther King Jr. followed the teachings of Jesus. And he embodied Jesus' way of radical compassion. Through an extraordinary act of compassionate intervention, King saved a man from certain beating. He also prevented an escalation of violence that likely would have sabotaged a nonviolent campaign in Birmingham before it even started. King's intervention was only possible, however, because of his capacity to remain grounded even in extremely reactive circumstances. Many issues could have provoked a punitive or retaliatory reaction from King: the arousal of fear when approached with menace, previous trauma in King's life, the instinctive rush of adrenaline and fury when physically assaulted. Instead, King retained his footing on solid ground and called a halt to the violence.

King maintained his internal equilibrium in three ways. First, King literally and figuratively caught his breath. In the chaotic swirl of escalating conditions, the emotions and passions of the moment did not hijack King. He took a breath. He found some way to relax despite his instinctive response to protect himself when threatened. In resisting impulsive actions, King remained well grounded. And from such internal stability, he could assess the situation calmly, firmly, and clearly.

Second, King's capacity to respond to an assailant immediately with compassion reveals that he was well grounded in the truth of his own belovedness. As I've mentioned before, we can only give of that which we have received. We can only treat another with dignity when we know our own dignity. We can only extend compassion to others when compassion has been extended to us. From a variety of sources—possibly his parents and family, his mentors and professors, his faith community, his prayer life—King internalized a profound sense of his own worth and his place within the Beloved Community for which he so fervently advocated. His internal reservoirs of love and compassion were already filled. His value did not depend upon the esteem of others. His sense of self-worth was so secure that it intuitively repelled the pounding lies of degradation in the fists of a racist attacker. Becoming grounded includes remembering our truth—we bear dignity as members of the Beloved Community. And no one can beat that truth out of us.

Third, King's capacity to extend radical compassion drew from a deeper well than his own. His commitment to nonviolent love as a means of transforming the hearts of his opponents was grounded in his faith in God. King embraced the man who attacked him not merely out of his own compassion but out of the sacred compassion in which all things are held and interconnected. Within this canopy of divine love, King believed even his attacker was one of God's children. Even his attacker was a member of the Beloved Community. For it is a community in which all people belong by virtue of our common ancestry in the Divine. King and his assailant were brothers. And both of them were held in love. Both of them were eternally embraced in the arms of God's compassion. For King, becoming grounded entailed sinking his roots deeply in the sacred soil that reveres and sustains all life.

We may seldom find ourselves in conditions as extreme as King did in Birmingham. We are, however, routinely knocked from our compassionate centers. We spend vast portions of every day reacting to persons and situations instead of responding in deliberate and connective ways. We are driven, rather unconsciously, by our fears, angers, anxieties, despairs, and passions that feed our addictive compulsions to work, eat, stay busy, or check out in front of the TV. A grounded internal stability often eludes us. In the cascading currents of busyness and reactivity, our capacities for care and connection can thoroughly erode.

When we find ourselves knocked off-center, we need a path that stabilizes and restores us. In the Compassion Practice, the first step of this path invites us to simply find solid ground. Like the three aspects King embodied in Birmingham, this ground solidifies underneath us when we catch our breath within the fury of reactivity and impulsiveness, when we remember and are emboldened in the truth of our belovedness, and when we root ourselves deeply in God's love—the spiritual source in which all of creation is part of the Beloved Community.

Getting Grounded When Knocked Off-Center

Nick, a friend of mine, described a peace vigil he once attended. After the invasion of Iraq, in the wake of 9/11, a Quaker group organized a silent witness for peace at a busy intersection in his town. Nick, a longtime practitioner and teacher of contemplative practice, arrived a few moments after the vigil began. The leader, a gentle elderly woman, approached him to share the parameters. Her lifelong commitment to Quaker activism nurtured a spirit of radiant calm that informed the design of the vigil. They gathered, she explained, to create an oasis of peace within the fever of war. Nothing more. They would merely act as a silent presence of care. Respect and courtesy would be extended to all who passed. But no words were to be uttered. They would embody peace, not debate it. Peace speaks for itself.

The woman cautioned Nick that this could be difficult—people might gesture, honk their horns, or shout their dissent. Nick assured her that as a teacher of contemplative practice, he knew how to be silent. He scrawled a sign that read *Peace for Our Children* and took his place on the edge of the sidewalk.

Within moments, right in front of Nick, a pickup truck stopped at a red light. The windows of the truck were rolled down, and talk radio blared from the speakers. The man inside fumed at the traffic, glared all around, saw Nick, and spat out, "Your children would be dead if we lived in Iraq."

Nick, seasoned contemplative that he is, spat right back, "Your children will be dead if we keep bombing innocent people."

"Don't talk about my children!" the man shot back.

"Don't talk about mine!" my friend rejoined. "I want peace for them all!"

"I'll show you peace!"

"Show me! I'm right here!"

A gentle arm wrapped around my friend's shoulder. He heard these words whispered in his ear: "That's okay. Just take a deep breath. Why don't we go for a little walk."

Nick and the elderly Quaker woman did walk. As the light turned green, the truck pulled away. And the peace vigil settled once more into silence.

———————

In an instant, reactive emotions can erupt from within us and hijack our consciousness. It happens to us all—even to contemplative practitioners. To be sure, anger can hijack us—a boss trashes the work we have labored on for weeks, a group cuts into the line we've stood in for hours, a pickup driver diminishes our children while we are standing at a rally—and fury ignites within us instantly. Other emotions hijack us as well. We have a presentation

to make, and anxiety burns through our bellies. Our child takes an over-
night trip, and fear all but paralyzes us. We hear the name of a lover who has
left us, and grief stabs us with rejection.

When hijacked by our emotions, we are gripped in their powers. Like
being swept downstream in cascading currents, the activated energy cours-
ing through us carries us away. At such times, no separation exists between
our impulses and our behaviors. We get mad, we yell. We are fearful, we
cower. We see the ice cream, we binge. We feel anxiety, we shut down. In
short, an impulse gets activated, and we act out in its power.

When we become activated, we need to wedge some space between our
emotions and our behaviors, between our impulses and our actions. We need
to find solid ground within the raging rapids of reactivity or the slow-moving
drift of unconscious routine—a place to stabilize ourselves within the possessive current and a secure vantage point from which we can lift our heads
and assess our situation.

We call such solid ground *awareness*. Becoming *aware* of our emotions, drives, and internal states instead of acting unconsciously consumed
by their power creates a space between impulse and behavior. For example, if my friend had noticed with nonreactive awareness the fury within
him that a truck driver's words triggered, a space of awareness could have
interrupted the impulse to yell back in defense. Within that space, we can
settle ourselves and then discern a more deliberate reply. This is the difference between *reacting* to life's circumstances and *responding* with grounded,
reflective self-awareness. Jesus demonstrates this routinely—resisting the
impulse, for example, to lash out at the lawyers who challenge him or even
at the soldiers who aggressively arrest him. Instead, he responds from a place
of grounded awareness.

How, when activated, do we create this space for self-awareness? Our
native wisdom provides an instructive starting point: Take a deep breath.
Regulating our breathing—slowing it down when it accelerates because of
reactivity or deepening it when it shortens through tension and anxiety—
grounds us in the moment. It actually restores us physiologically. Regulated
breathing activates the relaxation systems in our bodies. It stabilizes our
oxygen mixture, steadies a rapid heartbeat, calms tensed muscles, invigo-
rates endorphins, and dissipates toxic chemicals released in our bodies. Our
breathing literally recalibrates our bodies.[2]

The world's spiritual traditions recognize the power of our breath to ground us. Nearly every contemplative and cultural path to spiritual development begins with attention to our breathing. This is true for meditation. And it is true in the moments when we are activated by destabilizing impulses. Breathing is the most basic and efficient spiritual practice to restore and sustain a grounded posture. Anthony de Mello, quoting a Buddhist practitioner, puts it succinctly: "Your breathing is your greatest friend. Return to it in all your troubles and you will find comfort and guidance."[3] And the miracle of the body is that this friend is ever present, ever available. Our groundedness, quite simply, is a single breath away.

Sometimes a few moments of regulated breathing are enough to dispel an agitated state. Other times, we need to widen the gap between arousal and response—perhaps the emotion is too intense, the impulse to react goes too deep, or the situation's complexities cloud our vision. At such times, we need more space in order to emerge from the rapids of reactivity and solidify our footing on the banks of grounded perspective. Catching our breath means taking a break. We need a time-out. We need to settle the turmoil within. We can do this in multiple ways.

Change your location. Go for a walk, spend time in nature, find a quiet place to sit, take a drive, or take refuge in a sacred site—a chapel, mosque, temple, or monastery.

Engage your body. Do yoga, get a massage, take a bath, go for a run, ride a bike, throw clay, make music, dance, or draw.

Connect with a trusted person. Visit your therapist or spiritual director, talk with a friend, confide in a loved one, consult a mentor or spiritual teacher, seek counsel from a priest or pastor.

Perform a spiritual practice. Pray, meditate, journal, repeat a mantra, walk a labyrinth, or go on a retreat.

Such grounding activities give us space. They increase the distance between arousal and response. They bring calm to the agitated currents swirling within us. And with calm comes clarity. When a snow globe, shaken into a flurry of glitter, is stilled long enough for the glitter to settle, the dimensions of the landscape within become clear. Likewise, in taking the time to ground ourselves, our agitation can relax, and the underlying dynamics within our emotions, drives, and behaviors can come more fully into view. We may not be completely restored to our compassionate center, but we can at least see the tensions that need to be tended. We will have settled onto the stabilized ground from which compassion, both for ourselves and others, can be intentionally cultivated. The bottom line is, when triggered, don't just do something, sit there.

Remembering Ourselves as Beloved

Once we secure our footing on solid ground, we can take stock of the condition of our soul's terrain. Is the ground of our interior stability rich and fertile, the air crisp and fresh? Or is the ground arid and cracked, the air dirty and dry? Our capacities for compassion flow from the wellsprings of love within us. When we feel vital and valued, compassion seems ample and effortless. When we are harried and depleted, compassion feels burdensome and laborious. The well-loved child offers care freely; the deprived child becomes cold and withdrawn. We can only give from that which we have; we can only love with the love from within us.

We can replenish our wellsprings of love and compassion. We are, each one of us, wired for attachment. As much as food and water, we need love and care to survive. Without them, our spirits would wither. Our will to live would burn out entirely. That we function at all bears testimony that somewhere along the way we have been seen and validated. Persons in our lives recognized us for who we are. They affirmed our worth and beheld our beauty. They accepted us unconditionally. And the compassion they bestowed upon us kept alive the pulse of our humanity.

As a professor of spirituality at a school of theology, I have the privilege of attending graduation ceremonies. I was there when Raul Monroe received his diploma. Everyone knew Raul at the school. An openly gay man, he was graced with a religious tradition, the Metropolitan Community Church, that celebrated his identity and welcomed his ordination. Comfortable with his orientation, he founded the Gay and Lesbian Center on campus. He prepared for a ministry with the sexually marginalized, and he befriended with disarming affability persons who spanned the entire theological spectrum. The school community treasured Raul and was proud to celebrate his courageous vocation.

I was not so sure his father concurred. The moment I saw him, just before the ceremony, I felt uneasy for Raul. His father wore dark jeans, a black leather biker jacket, and a bandanna covered in skulls. Moreover, the man looked mean. Large and muscular, he seethed with a defiant scowl like a barroom brawler ready to backhand and body slam any bookworm sissy who dared to doubt the trouble he could cause. I could only imagine the terror a gay child endured in a house haunted by such a hulking presence. He followed, seemingly unamused, as Raul led his mother to the front row seats Raul had picked out for his parents. Once there, the father enthroned himself and then glared dead ahead as if thoroughly regretting this obligatory moment of domestic responsibility.

The ceremony proceeded without incident. Names were read; diplomas were distributed; graduates filed by precisely as rehearsed. Nothing tipped off the outburst preparing to blow. The time came for Raul's row to rise and approach the platform. Raul ascended the stairs. The dean trumpeted his name. And with the volume of a mama bear's roar and the glee of a school kid winning a trip to Disneyland, Raul's father leaped from his chair with his fist outstretched and bellowed for the entire assembly to hear, "That's my boy!"

People who extend compassion to us act as guardians of our soul. John Makransky calls them benefactors, emissaries of love in our lives.[4] These people see, understand, value, and celebrate us. They offer us the inestimable gift of revealing to us the truth of who we are—we are worthy of love even in our shame, we are held with love even when we forget it, and our beauty is beheld even when we feel blemished. Though our journeys may leave us broken and burdened, we remain thoroughly beloved.

Such emissaries of love sustain our spirit. Receiving their love replenishes the reservoirs out of which our own compassion flows toward others. We receive their love by taking the time to remember them, acknowledge their gift, and savor the care they so graciously extend to us. We can do this in a variety of ways: meditating on their loving presence, writing about their acts of care, telling their story to others, placing their picture in a sacred place, expressing gratitude to them directly, or lingering in the grace of their memory. Whatever the method, drinking deeply from these restorative waters fills the well of compassion within us. To give love, we have to receive love. In receiving more fully the love given to us, we have more from which to give to others.

Some spiritual writers remind us that whispers of kindness and compassion are extended to us throughout each day—the courtesy of a stranger holding open a door for our passing, the smile of a friend from across the room, the hand that holds ours when our spirits are down, the loved one who cares how our day has unfolded. Often, these register only for a moment and then flow past us. Practices like the Ignatian Examen help us notice and savor these whispers of compassion.[5] They also help us recognize and reconnect with the Spirit of God whispering within them. These practices recognize that the soil of our soul becomes all the more fertile as these showers of kindness soak deeply within us and collect into the pools of our interior reserves.

We can also be our own guardians of compassion. Often we neglect the act of self-care, and our souls and loved ones pay the price. Heightened reactivity is a symptom of a depleted and undernourished soul. Recognizing when our souls are weary and replenishing them restores our capacities for staying grounded within the cascading crosscurrents of our lives.

We rekindle our interior vitality through activities that leave us refreshed and energized, more alive and available—shooting hoops, going skiing, rock climbing, writing a poem, preparing a feast, dancing, painting, planting a garden, playing the guitar, playing with children, spending time with our loved ones, and so on. Cultivating our vitality solidifies our center. When fully alive, we are less reactive. Paradoxically, self-care increases our care for others. Loved and alive, we have love to lavish on those around us.

Knowing Ourselves as Beloved

For Christians, our breath intimately connects us to the sacred and sustaining life-force of the universe. In Hebrew (*ruach*), Greek (*pneuma*), and Latin (*spiritus*), the words for *breath* all refer not only to our literal breath but also to the animating life energy of the human spirit and—more profoundly still—to God's Spirit as well.

Jewish scripture particularly underscores this. Our breath, the Hebrew Bible suggests, flows from the very breath of God. God creates humanity when God breathes the sacred breath of life into the mud-formed being of the first human. And God's continuous breathing sustains our lives each moment. If God's breath were held, humanity would perish. (See Genesis 2:7; Psalm 104:29.) Indeed, some associate the Hebrew letters for God's name, YHWH, with the pattern of breathing—*Yod* (inhale), *Heh* (pause), *Vav* (exhale), *Heh* (pause).[6] If spoken aloud, God's name would sound like breath. Breathing itself is a prayer, one we have been praying since the moment of our birth.

Catching our breath, then, deepens our connection with God. It settles us into the stilling, grounding, restorative presence that holds and sustains all living things. This life-bestowing presence permeates our existence. It envelops our world, and it ebbs and flows into our deepest core. "Where can I go from your spirit?" the psalmist writes, "Or where can I flee from your presence? If I ascend to heaven, you are there; if I make my bed in Sheol, you are there" (Ps. 139:7-8). Paul likewise observes that "neither death, nor life, nor angels, nor rulers, nor things present, nor things to come, nor powers, nor height, nor depth, nor anything else in all creation, will be able to separate us from the love of God in Christ Jesus our Lord" (Rom. 8:38-39). God is the very sustaining presence in whom "we live and move and have our being" (Acts 17:28). As Anthony de Mello suggests, "The atmosphere is charged with God's presence. Inhale God as you would inhale air."[7] Or as the poet Kabir sees it, we are as immersed within God as fish within the sea.[8]

This sacred presence, as Jesus proclaims, is not neutral toward us. Connecting with God and resting in God's love provides healing and revitalization. God's presence has a pulse that beats to the pulse of compassion. In God's presence, we feel known, held, loved, and celebrated. God's face is not a face of judgment, aloofness, or punishing strictness but of infinite understanding, radical acceptance, and extravagant care.

Jesus experiences this God directly. According to each Synoptic Gospel, Jesus has a mystical encounter at his baptism that so pierces him, it inaugurates his earthly ministry and encapsulates the vital heartbeat of his spiritual teaching. As he rises from the cleansing waters, Jesus hears God speaking to him, "You are my Son, the Beloved; with you I am well pleased" (Mark 1:11).

Stephen Mitchell suggests the poignancy in this declaration when he notices that townspeople refer to Jesus as "the son of Mary" (Mark 6:3). In Jesus' culture, men are known as the sons of their father. In fact, children without legitimate fathers during this time are deemed *Mamzerim*, the excrement of the community. Calling Jesus "the son of Mary" is the cultural equivalent of a disdaining epithet, branding him as illegitimate, a bastard, the son of a wanton woman. Imagine, Mitchell surmises, the shame seared into the depths of Jesus' being when his very name—whether shouted or whispered in secret—betrays his stained identity as a person without a father, as a person without any kind of cultural worth whatsoever. Then imagine, Mitchell continues, the healing, the cleansing, the soaring restoration when God says to Jesus, "I am your father. You are my son. In you I have no shame, only delight. You are my beloved. You are held in my eternal embrace. Your worth is grounded in me."[9]

This is the God that Jesus knows, follows, and teaches: a God whose compassion and care transcends the shame-filled lies of the world, a God whose care can be known as intimately as water washing away our stains, a God whose voice calls us by our true name—children of God and heirs of a sacred lineage of love. Jesus knows this God intimately. He calls this God *Abba*—Daddy. And he teaches that the face of this tender and adoring Parent gazes upon all of humanity with eyes of infinite and unequivocal love. We see this face in the ecstatic father running to welcome a prodigal son back home. We see it in the adoring attentiveness of a parent who counts every hair on a child's head. (See Matthew 10:30; Luke 12:7.) We see it in the smiling delight of a caretaker beaming at our beauty like the flowers flourishing in the field. (See Matthew 6:28-30; Luke 12:27-28.) We see it in the grieving pathos of Mary as she holds her son's slain body in her lap.

The sacred breath, the divine presence, the face of God that beholds and sustains all life does so willingly, benevolently, generously, and delightedly. And in the same way that our bodies without breath would deteriorate and perish, so too would our spirits wither and die without a sustaining connection with the vitality of God's love. Without compassion, the soul decays.

During seminary, I served as a student intern at a church. Early one Saturday morning, I met a young boy, maybe twelve years old, sent by his mother to fetch a pastor. The night before, his brother had shot himself. I went with the boy. For several hours, I sat with his mother in wordless grief. Then as I was leaving, the boy, Joey, begged a ride back to the church. We sat in the parking lot, the morning still grey, as Joey laid bare some of his pain.

As Joey spoke to me, I began to understand that Danny, sixteen years old, was not only Joey's big brother but also Joey's only loving refuge in a house with a violent and addicted father and a mother so depressed she could not leave her bed to prepare meals for her sons. Joey spoke of many cherished memories of his brother. Then he shared words that still stay with me: "I want to ask you something," he said. "Something happened a few months back that I have been wondering about. Dad came home really ripped, ready to beat up anybody in his sight. Danny and I ran out of the house and down the hill. We got ourselves a couple of sodas at the store and hung out at the park. It was nighttime, and the two of us just sat there, waiting until we thought it was okay to go back. We didn't talk much. We just looked up at the stars.

"All of a sudden, this flying star just shot by, and the two of us started wishing upon this star." And Joey described a litany of wishes—two boys, back and forth, Danny, the older, leading; Joey, the younger, responding in kind.

"I wish I could play baseball like Willie Mays."
"I wish I could pitch like Juan Marichal."
"I wish I had a brand-new car."
"I wish I had a ten-speed bike."
"I wish Regina had the hots for me."
"I wish Suzie would leave me alone."
"I wish Dad would stop hitting everybody."
"I wish Dad didn't drink so much."
"I wish that Mom were happy."
"I wish that she would cook us dinner."
"I wish that Mom didn't need me so much."
"I wish that she would talk to me."
"I wish that Dad were dead."
"I wish that Mom would clean his clock."
"I wish that I were a long, long way from here," Danny mused.

As Joey described it, he did not offer a response to Danny's last wish. It was as if Danny really were a long, long way from there. But then Danny continued. "You know what I wish?" he asked. "I wish that I could fly. And if I could fly, I wish that I could fly right up into heaven. And I would fly right up to where God is sitting, and do you know what I wish? I wish that I could look straight into his face, and he would look back at me and smile." Then he took his empty soda bottle, threw it against a concrete wall, and spewed, "But the bastard would probably turn his back."

Joey turned to me on that grey Saturday morning and asked, "What I want to know is, was Danny right? I mean, I know we can't, but if we could. If we could fly and see the face of God, would God smile at us or just turn his back?"

————

Joey gives voice to a longing that echoes from the deepest shadows of our souls. If we could stand face-to-face with God, would God be cold and capricious or welcoming and benevolent? For Joey—and ultimately for Danny as well—it was a question of life or death. They knew a soul cannot long survive a certainty that God's face would scorn and disown it.

Joey's question haunts us as well. In regions so dark we seldom plumb them, a chilling uncertainty waits. At the rock bottom of life and eternity, in the presence of the sacred foundations of the universe, is our pain seen and held, are our cries heard? Are we, though bruised and battered, truly beheld as beloved?

The questions echo deeply. Deeper still lies the truth. In the bedrock of our soul we know. We have glimpsed this face of God. And with eyes filled with tears for the world, it is a face of infinite compassion.

In spectacular, unforgettable, mundane, and profoundly tender ways, the sacred compassion that sustains our world has touched our lives. We have glimpsed it—in the eyes of a loved one who sees our shame and treasures us anyway, in the kindness extended to us and to our families in times of immobilizing grief, in moments of mystical oneness with the beauty of creation, in the laughter of children, in the falling of snow, in the glistening of stars, in the innocence of a newborn's eyes. In each of our lives, moments of heightened connection amaze us with wonder and envelop us with wordless grace.

These moments are sacred. They are portals of presence, icons through which we catch sight of God's presence, which permeates the universe. And when we immerse ourselves in such moments, we sense it. We are not alone in the world. We are beloved. We are held not just in the care of our companions but also in the infinite love of God, whose regard for us is abundantly self-evident.

This is the truth. This is the ground of Christian compassion. And when standing firm on this rock of care, we have no doubt. We know precisely how to answer the poignant question of a boy haunted and alone.

Joey, if you know nothing else, know this: Wherever you find yourself before the face of God—whether in heaven, on earth, or in the living hell of a violent home—God will be smiling toward you with radiant delight, so pleased and proud to see you.

We increase our capacity for compassion when we stay grounded in the sacred truth of our belovedness. So often we forget. We start believing the lies that we are unworthy of love. We seek our value in our work, wealth, physical appearance, and in others while internally, the longing lingers. We long for the face of God to turn toward us with care.

The path of compassion invites us to remember that our belovedness is as secure as the air we breathe. It is the ground on which we have our being. God is smiling at us even now. Remembering, reconnecting with, and rooting ourselves deeply in God's loving presence reminds us of the truth of our sacred belovedness. Being born again is being born from this womb—the womb of God's compassion.

We deepen our connection with this compassionate presence in various ways—prayer, meditation, solitude, retreat, worship, ritual, fellowship, and community. Jesus retreats regularly to the mountains and seashore where he savors his oneness with God's love. Many reconnect with God by remembering and savoring the sacred moments that have graced them throughout the course of their lives.

Regardless of the practice, the invitation remains the same. We can return to the ground of infinite compassion, behold our face as beloved, and breathe this love into every fiber of our being. In doing so, we leave replenished, loved, and alive, bearers of love for our world.

The Sacred Source of Compassion

When I was a graduate student in spirituality, I met a man who knew how to ground himself in the sacred source of compassion. I was in need of spiritual replenishment, so I paid a visit to the local monastery at the edge of town. It was early when I drove through the gates. Instantly, I entered a world both still and mystical. I drove along the road and parked beside a '64 Rambler. I found the chapel and entered through the front door. The altar was already set—candles lit, a draped plate of bread, a chalice filled with wine. Weekday

Eucharist was about to commence. I stepped into the sanctuary, and that is where I first met Harry.

Harry was an elderly gentleman sitting alone about halfway toward the front. He wore clothes that looked like they had been bought at a thrift store—a tattered tweed jacket, a wrinkled white shirt, a clip-on tie inside a V-neck sweater. Most distinctive, however, was this stranger's posture: He had turned around and was beaming in my direction. It was as if he knew me, as if he was waiting for me—like he was the host of this party, I was the guest of honor, and he was so glad I had finally arrived.

Having no idea who he was, I simply smiled back, sat on the chapel's opposite side, and ignored him during Eucharist. When Mass was over, he grabbed my arm, and we chatted as we walked toward our cars. So began our daily ritual.

I learned his name, Harry, and that he was eighty-three years old and a retired telephone repairman. He and his wife raised two boys on a working-class salary. He was proud of them both—proud that they went to college and both became doctors. Harry lived alone. Some fifteen years earlier, his wife had died after forty-seven years of marriage. Every day after Mass, Harry would drive to the retirement home on the far side of town where he would spend the morning talking sports and playing checkers, listening to Sinatra, and gossiping with the women there. He never went empty-handed; he always brought donuts, turnovers, or bear claw pastries—unless it was a special occasion, in which case he would bring his legendary seven-layer cake. Rumor had it nobody could bake a cake like Harry's seven-layered masterpiece. Harry, quite simply, was one of the most charming people I had ever met.

One spring morning, I asked him a question. "Harry," I began, "every day I come to Mass, you're already here. You're always smiling and engaged. It's clear how important this is to you. What about the Eucharist is so meaningful that you make it the center of every day?"

Harry cocked his head, leaned forward on his cane, and stared into the distance. "I don't know," he mused after a spell, "I guess it just feels right somehow." And then, almost as if he were changing the subject, he said, "Say, did I ever tell you about my fortieth wedding anniversary? Man, was that something else. The missus and me, we'd been married forty years, and we were busting to do something special. The boys were away at college, so it was just the two of us. We dug out our best clothes from the closet, got all dolled up, and drove an hour all the way to the Jersey Shore, looking to find the best restaurant around. No Denny's for us, no sir. We wanted something classy. And as it turned out, we found something even classier than we knew existed: a restaurant that's only open for dinner. Can you imagine? Denny's is open twenty-four hours a day—you can get a Grand Slam for breakfast at two in the morning. Not this place. Only open for dinner. Now that's classy.

"But we didn't know that at the time. We just drove up in front of this fancy-looking place on the ocean and walked in. There was this man all dressed up in a tuxedo by the door, and he asks if he can help us. I say, 'Sure, we've come here for dinner. We'd like a table for two.'

"He says, 'That's fine, the only problem is, it's a quarter to six, and we're not open yet.'

"'You're kidding,' I say. 'You're a restaurant, right?'

"'That we are, sir,' he says. 'But here, we only serve dinner.'

"I'm thinking to myself, *Now this is a classy place.* So I say, 'Well, okay, is there somewhere we could sit and have a glass of wine? You see, today's our fortieth wedding anniversary, and we've come to celebrate.'

"And just about then, the owner of the restaurant walks by, overhears us, and says, 'You two been married for forty years?'

"'Sure have,' I say.

"'Get outta here, forty years today?'

"'Yes sir. And ready to do forty more.'

"'Well, come on in,' he says. He takes off our coats, and in we go.

"Man, you should have seen this place. It was like walking into paradise. All the tables had white cloths and crystal wine glasses and four or five forks and spoons lined up next to the china. They had plants coming out of the ceiling and a grand piano so shiny you could see your reflection in it. They even had a sculpture made of *ice*. I'm telling you, this place was classy. The owner, he takes us to this big round table by the window—the best seats in the house—helps us into our chairs, and says he'll be right back. Well, me and the missus are still figuring out what all the forks are for when he comes back with the guy in the tuxedo, a bottle of champagne, and four glasses.

"'This is on the house,' the owner says, 'We're going to have a toast. Tonight, we celebrate forty years of wedded bliss.' Well, he's working the cork off the bottle when one of the waiters walks by. 'What's going on?' he asks. 'We aren't even open yet.'

"The owner says, 'These two have been married for forty years.'

"'Get outta here,' the waiter replies, 'Really?'

"'Yeah,' the owner says, 'go get yourself a glass.' He runs off and another waiter walks by.

"'What's going on? We aren't even open yet.'

"'These two have been married for forty years.'

"'Get outta here, really?'

"'Yeah, go get yourself a glass.' He runs off, and a waitress walks by.

"'What's going on? We're not even open yet.'

"'These two have been married for forty years.'

"'Get outta here, really?'

"'Yeah, go get yourself a glass.' Then a busboy comes, a few more waitresses, and more waiters too with more glasses and more champagne until there's so much commotion going on, the cooks hear us way back in the kitchen. This guy with a chef's hat leans out the door and hollers, 'What's going on out there? We're not even open yet.'

"'These two have been married for forty years,' everyone replies.

"'Get outta here, really?'

"'Yeah, go get yourself a glass. Get the other cooks. Get everyone who's around. We're celebrating forty years of wedded bliss, and everybody's part of the toast,' the owner says.

"The next thing you know, there's about thirty people standing around our table, some of them wearing tuxedos, some of them in jeans and aprons, all of them with a glass in the air as happy for us as if we were family. And you know what, they didn't even know our names. I tell you what, that was one classy place."

In that moment of telling his story, Harry had come alive, radiant in this memory when strangers gathered around a table to celebrate love and marriage. All I could think to say was something pretty silly. "Gee, Harry, those are the moments that really warm your heart, aren't they?"

He paused for a bit, still recalling the sacred waters of that toast. Then he looked up at me and said, "Warm your heart? No. Those are the moments that keep me alive." Then after a few moments, he spoke again. "Tell me something," he said. "You're a seminary student. Do you think heaven will be like that?"

This time I knew just what to say. "Harry," I said, "I think heaven is going to be *exactly* like that."

"I hope so," he said. "I hope so." And with that, he settled into his car and drove across town to share a few hours with a different group of strangers whose lives he felt moved to toast.

Harry knows. He has glimpsed the truth of who he is. A simple telephone repairman, he is welcomed at the table with patrons of classy restaurants. His forty-year, working-class love is worthy of champagne with strangers. Staying grounded in this truth, his wells of compassion for others are abundant and overflowing. He becomes the gracious host to spiritually depleted seminary students and elderly residents of a retirement facility, welcoming others to the table of life where they too belong.

Harry replenishes these springs each morning through the spiritual practices that sustain his connection with God. He remembers the truth of his and others' belovedness in a Catholic monastery's early morning quiet, in the stories of grace he shares, and in the bread and wine of the eucharistic meal laid out for all to partake.

For Harry, this is only appropriate. For him, that moment of grace in a Jersey Shore restaurant provided a window into the sacred compassion that holds and sustains all life. Harry had a peek at heaven. A wedding toast shared amongst strangers was a glimpse of the feast of life to come. It is a feast where all are invited and welcomed—racist assailants and civil rights leaders, hotheaded truck drivers and reactive peace activists, biker dads, abused boys, aproned dishwashers, tuxedoed maître d's, and telephone repairmen. It is the feast of the Beloved Community, a feast that celebrates the sacred love in which all lives are worthy of toasting. This is the ground that feeds compassion. This is the ground that holds us all. This is the ground that keeps us and the world alive.

GETTING GROUNDED

Connecting with Your Breath

1. ***Find a rhythm of breathing.*** Determine a comfortable posture—either sitting or lying on your back—then take a deep breath, inhaling from and into the deepest part of your belly. It may help to place your hand on your diaphragm and notice your stomach extending as you fill it with air. Hold the breath in for a couple of beats, and then exhale as much air from your body as possible. Inhale again, breathing air into a deeper part of your belly, hold it a moment, then exhale once more. After several such breaths, each one slightly deeper than the one before, allow yourself to settle into a gentle rhythm of deep breathing that nurtures an interior silence.

2. ***Connect with the breath's sacred energy.*** If it feels helpful, imagine that you are breathing in the Spirit of God with each inhale and breathing out anything that disconnects you from God with each exhale. As you sense the presence of God, you may want to imagine the Spirit as a color, a light, or a sensation such as warmth, peacefulness, or compassion. Allow each inhale to deepen the sense of the Spirit permeating your body and soul.

3. ***Breathe the Spirit throughout your body.*** As you continue to breathe, become aware of your body one part at a time. Breathe God's Spirit into that part with each inhale and allow the energy to soothe that part in whatever way feels right. Begin with your toes, breathing in God's Spirit through your feet. Continue breathing in God's Spirit through your ankles and calves, your thighs, your groin, your lower back, your belly, your heart, your arms and hands, your shoulders, your neck and throat. Continue with your mouth and jaw, your ears, your eyes, your skull and brain, and around your scalp and head. Notice if any part of your body

remains in need of God's Spirit for whatever reason and breathe in this energy around that part, continuing to do so until you feel settled in an abiding sense of sacred connection.

4. ***Rest in contemplative presence.*** Allow yourself to rest in this sense of inner stillness anchored by the steady rhythm of your continued breathing. When you become distracted by a thought, feeling, or bodily sensation, allow the distraction into your awareness and breathe God's Spirit upon it until it relaxes, settles, or dissipates.

5. ***Return.*** When you are ready to emerge from this meditative space, invite God's Spirit to continue to sustain your breathing. Whenever you feel reactive, impulsive, or otherwise disconnected from your sacred center, pause for a moment and allow a few deep breaths to return you to a sense of settled presence.[10]

In the Moment

Over the course of your day, break the ongoing stream of your natural reactions to the world by simply taking a few breaths and noticing them. Breathing is a foundational grounding exercise and the basis of all the practices that follow. Pause and notice your breathing especially when you find yourself particularly triggered in any way.

GETTING GROUNDED

Remembering Sacred Moments

1. Take several deep breaths, and then settle into an interior silence.

2. Like thumbing through a photo album of your life, become aware of various moments in your life or the past week that felt sacred or expansive to you—moments of life, love, joy, wonder, or heightened connection. These may be intense and unforgettable moments or simple and mundane whispers of presence and connection. Of the various moments that come to you, allow one to emerge as the focus for the rest of this exercise.

3. Remember this moment by returning to it in your imagination.

   > Recall what was going on in your life at the time, where you were, and who accompanied you.

   > Reexperience the sensory details of the moment—the sights, sounds, smells, tastes, and bodily sensations.

   > Remember what seemed sacred or expansive about the moment and how this expansive presence felt.

4. Allow this sacred presence to swell once more within you. For as long as it feels right, rest in and savor this presence. Think of a symbol that embodies the essence of this presence—a healing light, Jesus, Mary, or a symbol of the Spirit.

5. In preparing to conclude this practice, discern if God is inviting you to allow the grace of this experience to extend into your daily life.

In the Moment

Find a tangible object or symbol that reminds you of one of your sacred moments. Carry this in your pocket or on a chain around your neck. Throughout your day, take a breath, remember this object, and be aware that God's presence accompanies you at all times.

Chapter 3

Taking Our PULSE

Cultivating Compassion for Ourselves

At eight months old, my son, Justin, took in everything. He loved to perch himself on the edge of his stroller, like a baby bird looking out from a nest, and scan every movement that played out before him.

One day Justin was posed this way while I walked him through a St. Louis mall. As the rest of the family shopped, I meandered with him among the folks crowding the mall's corridors and courtyards. Tired of walking, I leaned against a concrete planter and pushed Justin back and forth while he observed everything from his stroller perch.

While lingering there, I noticed a woman, perhaps retirement age, coming down the corridor toward us. Obviously upset, she defiantly plowed through the crowd, shopping bag clutched in one hand, a handbag in the other. People scurried out of her way as she barreled along. I was sure a straggler could get mowed down in her stride. I had no idea where she was heading or by whom she had been wronged, but I feared for the unsuspecting soul who dared get in her way.

What I did not notice was that Justin was watching her too. His wide-eyed look was befuddled, and he gazed straight at her as she beelined through the crowd. As she got closer to us, her head twitching in agitated fury, she did not break stride, but her scowling eyes glared sideways and locked onto Justin's. Justin's eyes, still wide with wonder, looked unblinkingly back into hers. And then he did the most amazing thing. He smiled. And with his smile, I watched as all of the hardness of that woman simply melted away. She let out a sigh, put down her bags, sank to her knees, and for several minutes, gave herself to giggling play. She tickled his toes; Justin grabbed for her glasses. Both of them cooing, ahhing, and glowing in delight at the beauty they beheld in each other. They were radiant. They were glorious. They were restored into the wonder of what humanity looks like when fully alive and flowing with love.

After several minutes, the woman looked up and noticed me. She mused a moment and then offered simply, "God bless him. And God bless you too." And with that gesture of goodwill, she grabbed her bags and walked away.

———————

Jesus teaches a path of personal restoration. For him, such restoration flows from the heart. As he insists when speaking to the fanatically devout Pharisees, we cannot measure our relationship with God by the perfunctory practice of religious rituals or the severity of our moral exactitude. Instead, we measure it by having a heart that beats at one with God's. Love and virtue grow naturally from a healthy heart like good fruit from a flourishing tree. Likewise, irritability and spitefulness, even viciousness and violence, grow all too easily from a damaged heart like bad fruit from a rotten tree. (See Luke 6:43-45.) Restoration transforms a hard heart into a supple one.

A supple heart beats to the pulse of compassion. It is a heart centered on God. It is soaked in God's extravagant compassion and immersed in a cosmic sense of its belovedness, so much so that any hardness softens, any depletion becomes replenished, and the pounding beat of fury and disgust relaxes into the steady pulse of care. When our hearts beat freely with compassion, we are restored. Our true face shines once more. Acts of kindness, care, connection, and delight flow easily and organically. Once more, we are radiant in the image of God.

Sometimes acting compassionately feels as instinctive as a child smiling spontaneously at a burdened and ill-humored shopper or as abounding as a rejuvenated woman blessing a baby and the parent behind the stroller as well. All too often, however, our hearts beat to impulses far less tender. A neighbor boasts of an Ivy League-bound grandchild, and we seethe with annoyance and inferiority. A loved one comes down with a case of bronchitis, and we groan with resentment and exhaustion. A salesclerk with attitude treats us discourteously, and we become the enraged shopper fuming through the mall. Compassion often requires cultivation. Damaged hearts require healing. We need a path that leads us to the face of love that restores us to ourselves.

The great secret of compassion is that this face is hidden within us.

Our Compassionate Core

The cultivation of compassion is really a process of recovery—of retrieving an inherent capacity that has become, either in the moment or over time, buried and obscured. Jesus' knowledge, which is grounded in the Hebrew scriptures, tells him that each person is created in the image of God—a God of infinite and extravagant compassion. (See Genesis 1:27; Exodus 34:6.) This image dwells unmarred within each soul. As such, we know how to care. We are wired for connection. We are born to love and to be loved. In truth, our deepest core is naturally compassionate. This compassionate core is our true self—our true face. We are most fully human when we live from this essence. We are most fully our true selves when we love.

The woman in the mall demonstrates this idea. When she is restored to herself, the burdens of fury having fallen away, care and connection flow freely and abundantly. She does not need to coax herself to be compassionate through willpower or spiritual practice. Once the hardness of her distress eases and washes away, she experiences care and connection. She returns to the truth of who she is. Her face beams once more. She is herself again, an inherently compassionate self.

We all have moments when we see persons, perhaps children, hurting, lost, or in tears, and our hearts spontaneously go out to them. We are moved by their pain, and we yearn to ease their suffering. Or we see radiant and alive persons—teenagers dancing, playing music, scoring goals on a soccer field—and we delight in their beauty and bliss. In such moments, something feels right inside of us; we feel in harmony with our human essence. We might even say to ourselves, *Yes, this is me. I'm being true to who I really am.* Conversely, should we rush by the whimpering child in our haste to meet our daily demands or disparage the teens indulging in activities that bring them joy, something feels off inside us. Our actions feel uncharacteristic, and in hindsight we might think, *I wasn't really myself that day.*

Psychologists such as Carl Jung and Richard Schwartz and mystics in the tradition of Thomas Merton refer to this enduring essence of humanity within us as the "Self."[1] Our Self is our true nature and the ground of our being. It is the pulse of love beating at the center of who we are. Moments of care and connection allow our true Self to shine. Such moments, even in as mundane a place as a St. Louis mall, can seem transcendent. The dullness and hardness and disconnection that pervade our chronic busyness dissipate. We experience a heightened awareness, a grounded stability, an abundance of love and goodwill. The face of our humanity beams unmarred like a woman beholding a smiling baby.

This compassionate core dwells intact within every living soul. Our outer shells may be numbed by indifference, hardened into coldness, or distorted by fear and fury, but the unblemished face of our true Self resides within each one of us. Like a pilot light of the spirit, our capacity to love lingers in the soul. As long as our hearts are beating, an impulse of care remains alive within us—a care both restorative and sacred. As the Quaker mystic George Fox observes, "There is that of God in everyone."

The enduring presence of a compassionate core—a Self that loves both freely and abundantly—suggests that the cultivation of compassion does not entail compelling a loving regard from ourselves. Rather, it is a process of clearing away the obstacles that prevent the free flow of our natural capacity to care. The act of cultivating compassion is similar to the legend about the famous Renaissance sculptor Michelangelo. As he hauled a slab of marble through the marketplace, a villager yelled out, "Michelangelo, what are you doing with that giant rock?" To which the sculptor responded, "You see a giant rock; I see an angel inside yearning to be free."

As we relax the fears, drives, passions, and hostilities that obstruct compassionate connection, our loving essence organically emerges from within. The face of our true Self reappears. As one Eastern proverb observes, "When the eye is unobstructed, the result is sight; when the ear is unobstructed, the result is hearing; when the mind is unobstructed, the result is wisdom; and of course when the heart is unobstructed, the result is love."[2]

Two Ways of Being in the World

But what about those tenacious obstacles? The affirmation that our truest essence is compassion—that care and connection flow naturally from us—does beg the question: What do we do when we are not feeling particularly compassionate? Truthfully, we spend vast portions of our lives disconnected from our compassionate core. Reactive emotions consume us—anger, fear, despair, and disgust. Internal voices harass us—voices of self-loathing, perfectionism, blame, or judgment. Behavioral impulses cause us to work, play, stay busy, or simply numb ourselves. If a true Self lies deep within us as an enduring capacity for grounded compassion, a self that feels false and disharmonious remains at the forefront of many of our everyday encounters.

Christian spiritual writers have referred to this variously as being enslaved to our lower nature, captive to a false consciousness or false self-system, or driven by the needs of the ego. Paul describes it as living by the flesh as opposed to living by the Spirit. (See Galatians 5:16-26.) Regardless of its characterization, we experience two qualitatively different ways of being in the world. We have moments when we feel grounded, centered, patient, and compassionate and other moments when we feel off-center, disconnected, moody, or impulsive. In these latter states, some psychic energy—an emotion, thought, fantasy, or behavioral impulse (what Ignatius of Loyola termed "interior movements" and what Richard Schwartz refers to as "Parts" of us)— arrives with such force that we are enmeshed in its agenda and carried away by its power. These states can endure. We may spend an entire day, for example, driven by the compulsion to work. Or they can come with the fury of a flash flood—a flare of anger at the sight of an offensive bumper sticker.

We classify interior movements into five categories:

Emotions (for example, anger, fear, lust, jealousy, and despair),

Internal monologues and inner voices (for example, voices of self-criticism, self-hatred, judgment, and perfectionism),

Behavioral impulses and desires (for example, to work, eat, have sex, veg out, and surf the Internet),

Images, daydreams, and fantasies (for example, daydreaming about a vacation while at work or fantasizing about getting revenge on someone who has hurt us),

Bodily sensations (for example, a dread in the pit of the stomach when going to a meeting with a supervisor, a heartache when thinking of a lost loved one, or a tensing of the body when considering the number of bills still to be paid).

These interior movements alienate us from our compassionate core. Indeed, they displace us from the grounded agency of feeling in charge of our lives. When they emerge, either instantaneously or in a slow advance, they take over the driver's seat of our consciousness. We are wheeled around at the mercy of their whims. We feel things we would rather not feel. We behave in ways we later regret. Compulsions that we cannot resist take over, and we find ourselves doing things we know are not constructive for ourselves or for the people around us.

These states feel all-encompassing. While we are enmeshed in them, the entirety of our personhood seems defined by the interior movements that have captured us. It feels as if we *are* the anger that consumes us, we *are* our addiction to food, and we *are* the incompetent frauds our self-hatred rebukes us to be. These are illusions. Our emotions, impulses, and inner voices are not who we are in our cores. They are charges of energy that have surfaced from the depths and hijacked our consciousness, at least for the moment. They mar the face of our true humanity. They disconnect us from the ground of our true Self. When they possess us, our compassionate Self seems like a long-lost acquaintance whose face we can no longer remember.

An example may be illustrative. Home from college, my son asks to borrow the car while I am at the office. This is fine, I assure him, as long as he picks me up on time—the previous summer he was perpetually late. After several sessions of spiritual direction, I'm feeling rather grounded and centered. I leave my office, greet some colleagues, and arrive at the curb precisely at six. Sure enough, my son is not there. Five minutes go by and then ten without so much as a phone call. The irritation begins to boil within me. Before I know it, I want to scream. I want to scold him, shake him, and shame him into respecting my very simple request. My heart no longer beats with the pulse of compassion; instead, it pounds with fury and outrage.

In an instant, an interior movement has taken over the wheel of my consciousness. I'm not driving the bus of my being anymore—anger is. And anger drives like a madman. When an interior movement appears within us, we usually do one of two things: we either act out or we resist. Acting out involves unconsciously surrendering to the possessive power of the movement's energy and demands—I may seethe and pace the sidewalk, playing and replaying an internal monologue (*I was absolutely clear what I needed from him! This happens every time! When is he going to respect someone else's needs?*), or I may launch an attack upon his arrival, fume in the car, and drill him about the repercussions of his obvious and chronic lack of consideration. Unconsciously acting out is a state of being enslaved to the interior movement taking over the driver's seat of our souls. Clearly disconnected from my grounded and compassionate core, I have *become* the movement itself. I *am* my rage. The energy of my fury has eclipsed the core Self of care and connection buried within me.

Resistance entails subjugating our reactivity or repelling it by sheer force of will. I may insist to myself that I'm really not upset at all, berate myself that I wouldn't be upset if I were more spiritually evolved (*You are a teacher of compassion after all!*), or perhaps simply minimize my feelings (*You really shouldn't be so impatient.*) and shrug off my anger so as not to ruin my evening. Resistance is a way of fighting the initial interior movement. In fact, it is a form of internal warfare. Rooted in shame, self-judgment, or discomfort because of the movement's existence within us, resistance seeks to banish it, discourage it, or overpower it so as to be rid of it altogether. This too is a state of disconnection from our grounded and compassionate Self. It is equally a form of captivity to an alienating interior movement—it is enmeshment, not in the anger itself but in the repelling energy that resists and reacts to the anger.

Both strategies lead to unsatisfying and counterproductive results. Acting out—far from resolving the conflict in question—only intensifies the disconnection I feel with my son and poisons my soul with toxicity in the process. And resistance is like trying to submerge a buoy underwater—the triggered emotion remains fully charged and keeps popping to the surface with dogged persistence. Both are forms of internal slavery, either to the psychic energy itself or to the counterenergy required to diminish the first. Neither brings healing. Neither resolves the issue. And neither restores us to our compassionate essence.

Taking the U-Turn

Jesus' spiritual path of compassion suggests a radical and counterintuitive alternative to acting out or resisting internal movements. Acting out and resistance both require that we focus on the external world—on the persons causing our distress or on the situations that provoke our reactions. We think that if we could change the circumstances, we could change the way that we feel. For example, *If Justin were always on time*, I rationalize, *I would never become angry. If he did not make me feel angry*, I continue, *I would not beat myself up with shame.* Instead of focusing our attention outward, Jesus invites us to turn inward, to take a U-turn, and to attend to the movements activated within ourselves. As Jesus puts it, when we see a speck in the eye of another, we should first tend to the logs in our own eyes. (See Matthew 7:3-5; Luke 6:41-42.) His words echo the airline instruction to secure our own oxygen masks before attending to other passengers.

The psychological observation behind this invitation is twofold. First, it recognizes that we can maintain a grounded Self-awareness free from enmeshment within *any* interior movement. When crosscurrents of the emotions and impulses that drive us take over—sometimes through acting out, sometimes resisting, sometimes in a high-pitched battle that goes back and forth—we are not in our right minds. We have lost our footing on the ground of our being. Our core Self, which could serve as our greatest resource, has been displaced from the driver's seat of our lives. When we allow our Self to take the wheel, it anchors us away from the storm of our cacophonous inner world, serves as the peaceful reprieve from the unceasing war between acting out and resistance, and frees us from the tyranny of our internal impulsiveness.

Christian contemplatives and explorers of the psyche recognize this ground of Self-presence that is free from enmeshment within our emotions, thoughts, and impulses. Thomas Merton refers to it as the Inner I; Quakers as the Inner Light; others as the seat of consciousness, the seat of the soul, or the seat of divine indwelling.

However named, the core Self resides in a qualitatively different sphere of consciousness than absorption within an interior movement. When grounded in the Self, we experience a state of *detachment* because we are disconnected from the possessive clutch of any internal movement.[3] It is also a state of *awareness* in which we notice movements within us without losing ourselves within them—the difference between "My heart is really pounding with fury" and the unconscious enmeshment of "I am so furious right now I could hit something."[4] We also can describe it as a state of *nonreactive, nonjudgmental openness,* of not resisting the presence of interior movements but allowing them to gently float on the untroubled surface of our awareness like clouds reflected on a glassy, still pond. The U-turn invites us to cultivate this interior space of grounded and detached Self-awareness. This open awareness cannot be defined as full-blown compassion, but it serves as a return to the ground of our Self whose abundant capacities for compassion wait to be tapped.

The second psychological observation behind the invitation to take a U-turn is that our discordant interior movements are rooted more within ourselves than in the outside world. Our reactions to the world primarily concern us. The fury at Justin, for example, that thunders through me shows signs of a sensitivity within myself and not a violation by him so inherently egregious it defies the reach of even a saint's compassion. We see that this sensitivity is mostly my own issue because countless others respond to tardiness with patience and understanding, perhaps even savoring the few moments of solitude. Yet I find such patience elusive. Further, the severity of my reaction tells me something. As Jesus so brilliantly recognizes, a mere ten minutes—a "speck" of tardiness, so to speak—causes a "log's" worth of indignation within me. Clearly something in my own soul requires tending and restoring. The invitation toward compassionate Self-restoration asks that I calm myself and recalibrate the erratic pulse to which my own heart races. Only then may I tend to the situation at hand from a more grounded and centered posture.

This insight—that our reactions to the world are primarily based in us—ultimately liberates us. The power to claim and retain our own humanity lies in us and not in others. Our responses to the world do not depend upon what other people do to us, even when they treat us in harmful and provocative ways. We can cultivate a grounded Self-presence so secure that like birds resting on electrical wires, thousands of volts of charged energy can course below us without eroding our strength and dignity. No one has the power to rob us of our Selfhood. Others can demean us, but they cannot dehumanize us. Our humanity belongs to each of us. And the path to claiming it requires compassionate attention to the turbulence within us.

Interior Movements as Cries for Compassion

Another radical realization textures the invitation to take the U-turn and tend the erratic movements within us, one with life-transforming potential. Every interior movement we experience—every emotional fluttering, mental monologue, imaginative fantasy, or behavioral impulse—is rooted in a cry of pain or a need straining to be heard. All interior movements bid for life. They attempt to protect us from a threat, to claim power or vitality, and to secure the love and connection on which our flourishing depends. An interior movement may become extreme, destructive, or relentless when something essential for our survival feels threatened and demands our attention. Such movements are fighting for our lives in the only way they know how. As Richard Schwartz observes, every movement within us means well and is rooted in some positive intention.[5] Or as Marshall B. Rosenberg says of extreme emotions, every tenacious interior movement is but the tragic cry of an unmet need.[6] Here are a few examples: pangs of jealousy at a colleague's new book may be the frustrated groans of the book within us aching to be birthed, an impulse to surf the Internet for hours may be the exhausted plea for some centered downtime, or a voice of relentless self-castigation may be the scream of terror at being rejected if we are unable to reach perfection.

Each one of these energies—jealousy, rage, compulsivity, self-castigation—wreaks havoc within our inner worlds and represents the wail of an unsoothed *fear* (of violation or attack, for example), an unsatisfied *longing* (for rest and renewal, perhaps), an *aching wound* still bruised (such as scars of abandonment or rejection), or a *gift* obstructed that cries out to be owned and nurtured (cultivating self-expression, for example, or claiming our personal voice). To be sure, their pleas can be painfully clumsy and tragically desperate. They come out as, "Why do her books always get so much press?" or "I'm never going to be good enough." The hidden cry underneath, however, says, *I'm in pain. Please, someone, see me.* Our interior movements bid for healing, wholeness, and integration. They serve as reliable barometers of what our souls need to survive and flourish in the world. They yearn to be heard, held, and healed. They are not our enemies; they are battered guides pointing the way to life. This is a revolutionary idea.

Normally we war with our inner movements. When not carried away by their possessive power, we judge them as bad or destructive and manage them through power of will or distraction. I feel shame for my anger at Justin and siphon it off by running a few miles or bingeing on Häagen-Dazs ice cream. Or I fear my anger's destructive power and push it away through interior scolding. In reality, this only intensifies my internal conflict. Emotions and drives elude any attempt to be handled. I might secure a short-term reprieve, but my anger returns in full force the next time Justin is ten minutes late—or if not Justin, a colleague, a partner, or a delayed airplane. Like a child who screams louder when ignored, these interior energies become more severe when their cry is unheard and their suffering dismissed. They long not for subjugation but for compassionate care.

This recognition opens the door for a radically new relationship with the movements that rage within us. Instead of fighting them with strategies of resistance, taking the U-turn invites us to listen with care to the cry of pain hidden within them. It invites us to do for ourselves what we would do for others. If friends came to us unnerved by persons who had left them waiting or beating themselves up after sniping at their children, we would listen with care and understanding. In the same way, we have the opportunity to listen to the agitated cries within ourselves. And when we do so, the suffering within those cries surfaces. We are moved. Compassion fills us up and flows from within. The face of care at our core emerges once more. And remarkably, as we extend this care to the turmoil within us, the interior stirrings relax, their deep needs make themselves known, and, in the attentive gaze of our compassion, they are healed and made whole.

This is genuine Self-compassion. Compassion flows from our true Self, and we extend that compassion to the cries of suffering clamoring within our own souls. The path of the U-turn restores the Self; it restores the heartbeat of our compassion.

Taking Our PULSE

How then do we cultivate such Self-compassion? How might I, for example, recalibrate the racing pulse of my anger at Justin to the pulse of compassion and turn my attention inward? The first step of the Compassion Practice invites us to catch our breath. We need to find a way to interrupt the rush of reactivity and regain emotional grounding. We can do so by taking a walk, playing music, meditating, or connecting with a confidant. Then, using my example, instead of scheming ways to change my son or even forcing a compassion for him that I do not feel, the second step of the Compassion Practice invites me to cast my gaze inward and take my PULSE.

Following the five components of compassion outlined earlier, I would start by *paying attention*. Paying attention involves cultivating a nonjudgmental, nonreactive awareness of whatever movement has been activated within us. Such awareness does not remain enmeshed in the movement or in any judgmental, reactive, or resistant countermovement. It simply acknowledges that one or more movements are present. This awareness settles us in the ground of Self-presence that is genuinely open to the movement and curious about why this movement is within us at all.

We can extend grounded Self-awareness to any interior movement—emotions like rage, lust, depression, and fear; internal voices of self-laceration and judgment; impulses to binge, work, commit acts of violence; fantasies of love, escape, or revenge. This Self-awareness trusts that at the root of every movement within us we will find a bid for life and a cry for care. And this Self-awareness holds all movements with a radical acceptance and welcoming spirit, both of which are open to understanding the cry hidden within it. Rumi's poem "The Guest House" describes this posture that opens the door of our Self-awareness and welcomes any interior visitor that comes, for each "has been sent as a guide from beyond."[7] If, in the course of paying attention, we do not feel open to a movement that is present—if, for example, we find ourselves judging it, handling it, afraid of it, or analyzing it—then we are enmeshed in another interior movement. So we cultivate a nonreactive, nonjudgmental welcoming awareness of *that* additional guest. And we continue until we ease into the space of genuine openness.

In the case of my reaction to Justin's tardiness, I notice that fury is present within me. Without fanning its flames or fighting its energy, I can simply be aware of this emotion's presence. I would also notice that shame, self-judgment, and an impulse to self-medicate on ice cream are activated within me. I would welcome them all into the guest house of my awareness. Each emotion means well; all are burdened with pain. I invite them to relax now that they have my attention. As I open myself to these emotions, I ease once more into the presence of my Self. I am in my right mind again. And from this posture of restored Self-presence, genuine understanding and compassionate connection become possible. Now I am in a place to listen more deeply to the cry of the fury within me.

Once we ground ourselves in Self-presence and are truly open to the interior movement, we then seek to *understand empathically* the suffering hidden within it. The movement itself cries out because something vital to our thriving feels threatened or at stake. Like an indicator light on a car dashboard, the interior movement signals that something needs our attention. Or alternatively, the movement is like the waving flag of a person in distress, frantic that his or her need be seen and tended. We cultivate empathic understanding through listening deeply to the movement until the source of its distress makes itself known. The distress within the frantic FLAG of an activated interior movement is rooted in one or more of the following:

F—*Fear.* The movement is terrified of an imminent danger—perhaps rejection, ridicule, violation, attack—and mobilizes to protect us from the threat.

L—*Longing.* The movement yearns for something essential to our flourishing—renewal, freedom, love, or life.

A—*Aching wound.* Pain from the past still stings and bleeds and, when triggered in the present, cries out to be held and healed. These wounds could come from shame, abuse, abandonment, or neglect.

G—*Gifts obstructed.* The movement holds the burgeoning seed of a talent or a personal capacity that has been denied and buried and is bursting to be claimed and nurtured into flourishing—the gift, perhaps, of our voice, power, tenderness, or art.

When we hear the source of the cry within the interior movement, something shifts inside of us. We are moved. An understanding dawns, and we think, *No wonder I respond, act, or feel this way.* We finally understand and soften; compassion rises from within.

What might surface as I listen deeply to the cry within the waving FLAG of my fury at Justin? I would hold the fury in my curious gaze and ask myself: What does my fury *fear*? For what does it *long*? What *aching wound* is tender and stung? What *gift* or strength has been stifled or discouraged and pleads to be claimed and nurtured?

Perhaps I would sense that my fury is rooted in a deep terror of being forgotten—ten minutes of tardiness feels like a lifetime of being abandoned and left alone. It may help to imagine my fury as a child or to allow a memory to materialize. One comes. The pain feels like that of a wounded boy—me at eleven years old—shivering in the cold because his preoccupied mother forgot to retrieve him from a swim meet in the next town over. I see the boy trembling in the dark, his back against the wall of a deserted recreation center. Beholding that boy moves me. No wonder I recoil when I feel forgotten. A neglected young boy has ached for years for someone to soothe his aloneness in the world and to heal his fear that he really deserved nothing more. I get it now. Understanding dissolves the fury and comes from the true face of my Self.

Understanding gives rise to *loving with connection*. Like a mother cradling her crying child, we offer care. We reassure the fears that terrorize from within. We hear the longings and heed their needs. We tend the inner child still aching and wounded. Our compassion makes room for the cry within until the suffering inside of us feels fully seen, heard, held, and healed.

As the suffering beneath my fury becomes more real for me, personified by this boy within me whose pain is still fresh, tender care rises up and flows through me. I want to assure the boy that he is alone no longer and wash away the lingering lies that he ever did anything to deserve being abandoned. I hold him. I let him weep. I let him know he will never be forgotten again. Not by me.

The care flowing within me comes from a deeper source than myself. It shimmers with the sacred compassion that comes from the heart of God. *Sensing the sacredness*, I know in my bones that God's heart breaks for this boy and enfolds him in eternal care. God's infinite compassion aches to seep into that boy and to bring him a healing certainty that he is forever held by love, forever seen and valued, even in a world where mothers are too wounded to remember their children alone in the dark. I invite God's love to surround the suffering boy within me—as Jesus, a breath of the Spirit, a healing light, or a symbol of God's presence. It comes. Jesus holds that boy in the dark. And the boy knows he is held not only in my compassion but also in the sacred source of all compassion. He begins to heal, his primal terrors are soothed, and his connection with God intensifies. In this space, we are united with the Divine. We are lover and beloved, giver and receiver, all at once. We are held in the womb of infinite compassion. And infinite compassion holds and heals all wounds.

Such compassion restores our lives. New life is birthed and yearns to be fully embodied. We may find that we now trust our worth, feel confident in our power, sense our belovedness and beauty, and are aware of the beloved beauty in others. *Embodying new life* recognizes the gifts and qualities budding within, and it longs to see them flourish. For me, I find that patience is growing within me—patience both for the bruises that continue to provoke my furies and for my loved ones who inadvertently brush up against my insecurities. In addition to this patience, I feel confidence in an enduring love that eases my dependency on others to assuage my sense of aloneness in the world. For the moment, my once erratic heart pulses with the heartbeat of compassion.

Paying attention, understanding empathically, loving with connection, sensing the sacredness, and embodying new life—the PULSE of compassion comprises these five steps. Our hearts beat to this pulse when restored to the natural essence of our core and caring Self. This Self-compassion flows from the essence of Self within us, and it extends to the suffering hidden within any interior movement whose cry wails from inside of us. Self-compassion heals, makes us whole, and connects us once more with the sacred compassion whose face gazes from the depths of creation, weeping for our pain and smiling at the beauty within us coming to life.

CULTIVATING COMPASSION
FOR YOURSELF

Welcoming Presence Meditation

1. Get grounded by taking several deep breaths and easing into an interior silence.

2. As your breathing continues, settle into an interior space that feels safe, grounding, peaceful, and receptive. You may want to imagine this space as a specific place, either real or imaginary, that feels welcoming and sacred. For example, you can imagine a living room, a quiet chapel, a meadow, a beach, a warm cabin—any place that soothes you, centers you, and fills you with the promise of sacred presence.

3. As you relax into this interior space, intrusions may invade the quiet. These intrusions may be emotions, thoughts, inner voices, fantasies, body sensations, urges, or any other interior movement that ripples into your inner calm. Instead of demanding that they leave, being carried away by their power, or judging yourself for their presence within you, welcome them as guests within your interior space. Here are some tips to assist you:

   > Refer to the intrusion in the third person. Instead of thinking *I am stressed right now*, think *Stress is present within me.*

   > Express a welcoming attitude toward this intrusion. *I see you anxiety. Welcome. I allow you to be present within me.*

   > Recognize the intrusion as a guest. *I trust you are here for a reason. I may not know what it is, but I trust that you come with a gift.*

4. Ask the guest to express itself as an image—perhaps as an object like a coffeepot, chattering teeth, or a hive of buzzing bees; perhaps as a person or creature. Then, in whatever way feels right, honor and preserve this guest by placing it somewhere within your interior space. Perhaps you wrap it in a prayer shawl and place it on an altar. Maybe you place it in a gift box and put it on a shelf to open later. You might invite the guest to sit in a chair next to you. Or you can choose any other way of honoring its presence and allowing it to remain until a later time when you will become more fully acquainted.

5. Return to a sense of inner peace and gentle presence, reconnecting with your breath as needed to still and center yourself. Whenever you notice an interruption in this state of relaxed presence, welcome and receive that interruption as a guest in the same way that you welcomed and received other intrusions.

6. Invite a sacred presence—Jesus, Mary, the Holy Spirit, or a healing light—to come and be with you and your guests in whatever way feels calming, healing, or restoring.

7. Before surfacing from this interior space, notice the gift you are receiving from the practice and allow that gift to flow throughout your entire body and extend into every part of your inner world.

8. In preparing to conclude this practice, discern if there is an invitation for how you might allow the gift of this practice to extend into your daily life.

(Note: This practice can be engaged through many different modes, of which interior meditation is but one. If you feel compelled, try this practice through other activities: writing, making a collage, drawing, working with clay, or playing music.)

In the Moment

Over the course of your day, when you become aware of an interior movement threatening to possess you (a strong emotion, a powerful impulse to act in a certain way, a relentless inner voice, a bodily sensation, or a fantasy that has gripped you), ground yourself by taking some breaths. Notice the movement that is flooding you by saying to yourself, *I notice that _____ is present within me. I greet you _____.* Place the movement somewhere safe and contained within yourself.[8]

CULTIVATING COMPASSION
FOR YOURSELF

Deepening Your Understanding of an Interior Movement

1. Recall one interior movement—a powerful emotion, a persistent inner voice, a compelling impulse—that has been a frequent companion in your life recently or one that has given you difficulty in the past.

2. Take a few minutes and personify this interior movement, perhaps imagining it as a child or some creature that embodies the feelings of this movement. You can do this in your imagination, by drawing it, or by finding a picture on the Internet.

3. Spend some time *paying attention* to this personified emotion. Extend to it a nonjudgmental and open presence of care that genuinely seeks to understand its experience. (Note: If you are not feeling open, nonjudgmental, and curious toward this interior movement, another interior movement has slipped in—so notice that movement and then invite it to relax until you genuinely feel open and curious toward the personified emotion.) Invite the interior movement to embody its experience by asking, *What gender would it be? How old would it be? What would it look like as it experiences this emotion (its facial expression, its bodily posture, its attire, and so forth)? What is it feeling and experiencing within the situation that activates it?*

4. Cultivate an *understanding* of the cry within the personified movement. Invite it to unearth its deeper suffering through whichever of the FLAG questions reveals its pain:

> ❯ What is your deepest *fear* underneath the movement?

> ❯ What is your deepest *longing* underlying it?

> ❯ What *aching wound* do you carry that remains sensitive?

> ❯ What *gift* that you are trying to give me feels stifled or discouraged?

5. After you have finished this interview, invite the personified interior movement to summarize what it has shared with you by filling in the following:

   Whenever I (the personified interior movement) get activated during the day, I need you to hear and understand _____. In short, I long for _____.

6. After you have finished this interview, think of a physical object that represents or symbolizes this persistent interior movement. Make sure the object is something you can carry with you for a few days (for example a coin, stone, button, bead, cross, acorn, ring, paper clip, or eraser).

7. Conclude your reflection by inviting a sacred presence—Jesus, Mary, a symbol of the Spirit, a sense of God's presence—to be with the personified interior movement in whatever way feels healing and life-giving.

IN THE MOMENT

Over the course of a few days, carry the symbol of the interior movement with you. At various times during the day, simply notice this object as a way of recognizing that this interior movement is a part of you that needs attention and care. Whenever you feel this interior movement becoming activated, tend to it with some variation of the following: Take a moment to breathe and ground yourself. Reconnect with the symbolic object that you are carrying. Notice that the interior movement is once more present by saying to yourself, *(The name of the interior movement) is here. I see you.* Ask the movement, *What do you need me to understand right now?* Assure the movement that you understand and will tend to its need. Invite the movement to relax and step to the side for now—perhaps returning into the object that carries it—until you are able to tend it more fully.

Chapter 4

Taking Their PULSE

Cultivating Compassion for Others

A friend of mine who works as a dance therapist attended a wedding reception. A small band played before a modest dance floor, and people clustered around the sea of round tables that spread throughout the reception hall. Sitting at one of the tables, she paused from her conversation and noticed an elderly gentleman in a wheelchair. He was threading his way through the tightly packed tables toward the nearly empty dance floor. Once he arrived there, he simply leaned back in his wheelchair and swayed back and forth to the music.

Something about the man moved her. My friend stood up, made her way to the dance floor, bent before the gentleman, and said, "Excuse me, sir. We don't know each other, but could I share this dance with you?"

With a wave of delight coming across his face, he said, "Why certainly, miss. It would be my pleasure."

For the next several minutes, the two of them danced. With grace and elegance, they glided up, down, and across the floor. Other couples moved to the side, those at the tables hushed and looked on, as these two twirled, rocked, and swayed as one to the rhythms of the music.

When the song ended, the audience applauded. The band members bowed in tribute, as well. The gentleman, still bright in the glow of the dance, looked at his partner and said, "Thank you, oh, thank you. It's been twenty years since I've danced. I used to be a dancer, you know. My how I have missed it. When I dance, I feel loved. When I dance, I feel the power of God lifting me up into life."

Jesus' way of radical compassion is not limited to grounding ourselves in God's compassion and cultivating a Self-compassion that stills and heals the turmoil within us. Like a heart that propels replenished blood cells to heal and renew a weary body, this spiritual path pulsates us into compassionate care toward others. As my friend reveals, such compassionate care restores both others and ourselves. It reconciles us to the love that soothes the soul and sustains the spirit. Through it, we move to healing rhythms. With the power of God, we are lifted up into life.

My friend's act, though spontaneous, embodied the PULSE of compassion. *Paying attention,* she noticed another human being—in this case, an elderly man in a wheelchair determined to get to a dance floor. *Understanding empathically,* she was moved by his yearning to move with the music, even if alone and of limited mobility. *Loving with connection,* a swell of care and generous regard filled her and flowed toward this man swaying by himself to the music. *Sensing the sacredness,* her care became a channel of a loving energy that hushed a room and lifted them all into life. *Embodying new life,* she yearned for and then celebrated the glowing vitality of a man who danced once more and felt himself beloved. To be sure, my friend's gesture of dancing with this stranger moved to the pulse of compassion.

The Precondition for Cultivating Compassion

My friend's compassion was rather instinctive. Such compassion for another can also be cultivated. The essential precondition, however, is that we are open to a compassionate encounter. When we are not open to a compassionate connection with someone—when we are feeling reactive, dismissive, frightened, overwhelmed, or even simply numb and distracted—an interior movement holds us in its grasp. Compelling a feeling of compassion at such times can seem fake and comes off instead as feigned civility or charity laced with our own agenda. In addition, it dismisses the cry of our interior movement and thus ignores the need or suffering hidden within it. This is internally contradictory. Coaxing a soft heart to care for another while hardening our hearts toward ourselves is, as previously mentioned, like straining to force relaxation. Something within us resists and digs in. This resistance reveals the unmet need or unhealed wound that continues to cry out from within us. When ignored, its suffering only intensifies, and it screams for attention in other ways—as compassion fatigue, a seething resentment, or a stomach churned to chronic upset. For the well-being of both body and soul, we must recognize and listen to these interior cries.

This may be what most distinguishes the way of Jesus—as distilled into the Compassion Practice—from other methods of cultivating compassion. When encountering another, if we do not feel open to connection, we must first turn inward and tend the erratic pulse within us. Metaphorically, we are caring for the logs in our own eyes before focusing on the speck in the eye of another. This in no way is meant to demonize the movements within us that resist compassion. On the contrary, these movements guide us on the path through which we are restored to our Self. They signal the needs and wounds within us that require care before we can relax into the core of compassion.

The key diagnostic tool to assess our readiness to cultivate compassion toward another is to ask ourselves, *Do I genuinely feel open to a compassionate connection with this person?* If we do not, we take the U-turn and notice the stirrings that have been activated within us. Like a skilled chiropractor assessing mobility and noting pain, we surface our antipathies and address the cries hidden within them. My vindictiveness toward another, for example, may be a plea for safety and protection. My numbness may be fatigue aching for renewal. My fierce busyness may be the panicked fight to keep from losing myself in chronic and ceaseless caretaking. In turning inward and taking the pulse of our activated states, a Self-compassion emerges that not only relaxes and satisfies our agitated movements but also forms the ground on which genuine compassion for another can be cultivated. We discover once more the capacities within us to truly love our neighbors with the same love with which we love ourselves.

Once we are restored to a grounded Self-compassion, we return our attention to the other person. Sometimes this is enough. Soothing the cries within our reactions may suffice to lead us to a place of care and understanding. Having tended the logs in our own eyes, we are able to see clearly again. Then, like my dance therapist friend, we may simply take notice of someone before us and feel an organic wave of affection filling and flowing through us.

Sometimes, however, more effort is required. We gaze at someone else and cannot help but see that a speck really is lodged within his or her eye. We are open to the person, but we are not necessarily moved by the person's presence or behavior. Cultivating a genuine compassion toward that person is still possible, and the process by which it is cultivated is informed by three core Christian understandings.

Other People Are Beloved by God

First, Jesus embodies a compassion that extends to all persons—sinners, centurions, the suffering, the self-righteous, and even toward those who conspire to crucify him. And his compassion is grounded in a God whose compassion extends to all as well. For Jesus, God resembles the herder of a hundred sheep who, so heartbroken for a single lost stray, would leave the ninety-nine safe in their fold to scour the wilderness for the one lost and alone in the night. (See Matthew 18:12-14; Luke 15:1-7.) God's love, like the sun, shines on the just and the unjust alike; like the rain, God's love falls on the good and the evil. (Matthew 5:43-48.) God's love extends to every being in creation. No matter how broken, marred, tortured, or twisted persons might become, God grieves their wounds, celebrates their joys, and holds them securely in the divine compassion that reaches into any swampland in which they may be ensnared. As the Jewish commentator observed, even while the Jews rejoice as the Red Sea closes to seal their escape, God grieves the deaths of the Egyptian pursuers, the work of God's hands drowning in the waters.[1] God weeps for the Iraqi soldier killed as much as for the slain American, the robbery suspect as much as the cop killed on duty. As the big-hearted bumper sticker generously bestows, "God bless the whole world. No exceptions."

Every being in creation is inherently beloved. God holds each person we meet in the course of our days and journeys—the person beside us when we wake in the morning, the barista serving us coffee, the officer directing cars, the motorist fuming at the standstill traffic—in the sacred love that sustains and restores all life. Like the parent who stops to behold a sleeping child, God gazes upon each person, valuing each one as beloved. As we hold others in the light of this love, our hearts open more fully toward them. And it deepens our connection to the compassionate God whose expansive reach extends even to those lost and on the margins of society.

A chaplain I know was visiting a hospital when he overheard two nurses talking. One was sharing that the police had shot a gang member who had executed a teenage girl. The gang member's death was imminent, but his heart was a match for a transplant uptown. The nurse listening was aghast.

"Who," she asked with disgust, "would want the heart of such a monster?" According to Jesus, God would. God's heart breaks both for the young woman so brutally slain and for the horrors that gave rise to the tortured soul that would do it. When our own hearts can hold such compassion, we become instruments through which God's love holds and heals the world. In the face of our compassion, the person we behold catches a glimpse of God's face. They see themselves in the truth: No matter what, they are and remain beloved.

Other People Bear the Pulse of Humanity

Second, as we cultivate our compassion toward others, we must remember that the pulse of humanity beats within the depths of everyone we encounter. Since each person is created in the image of God, the seed of a compassionate and intact Self dwells within every person we meet. However dim it may be, the steady ember of a true Self, an abiding capacity for compassionate connection, resides within every human heart—no matter how damaged or hardened that heart may become.

It beats even in a heart as damaged as Damian's.

Damian was an eighth-grader at an inner city school in Toronto. With multiple tattoos and piercings, Damian looked as tough as he behaved. He challenged his teacher and was incapable of focusing on his school work. He could not restrain his vocal impulses, and he was constantly on the edge of an angry outburst, even to the point of accosting other students if they got anywhere near him. His teacher understood the roots of his behavior. At four years old, Damian watched his father shoot and kill his mother. With his father in prison, his mother dead, and no other family members to take him in, Damian spent the next ten years tossed among over twenty foster homes and several government facilities. Over time, his rage and aggression became increasingly impossible for him to contain. Now an eighth-grader, he was one assault away from a permanent stay in reform school.

To his teacher's trepidation, Damian was present when Mary Gordon visited the classroom. Gordon, founder of Roots of Empathy, had a unique method for cultivating empathic connection. She brought an infant, along with the baby's parents, to class for the students to observe. Damian resented the intrusion. Scowling with annoyance, he studied the situation from a perch across the room. The other students spent the morning cooing with the baby on a blanket and taking turns holding her. After some time, the mother announced that the baby needed to nap. To everyone's shock, Damian came over and asked if he could walk the baby to sleep. The teacher tried to caution the mother, but the mother felt an intuitive trust.

Damian slipped into a Snugli and carefully strapped the eight-month-old child in place against his chest. An instinctive care kicked in. Like a seasoned and affectionate father, Damian pressed her close and softly rocked her in his arms while gingerly walking around the room. The baby glanced for her mother at first, but then sensed that she was safe. Drowsy, she closed her eyes and fell asleep. Damian grew wide-eyed with wonder. Careful not to wake her up but unable to contain his triumph, he nodded his enthusiasm to the others in the room and whispered to each one around, "Look, I got her to sleep. See, she's really sleeping."

Damian savored the moment, walking the room, cradling the child, and beaming for all who would see. When it was finally time for her to leave, Damian handed the baby to her mother. He caressed her head. He said good-bye. Then he turned to his teacher and asked, "Do you think if nobody ever loved you it's still possible to be a good dad?"

———————

Though Damian has been damaged by horror and hardened by heartache, he still carries an unmarred face of compassion. His true Self is fashioned in the image of God. This core and abiding Self contains an enduring capacity for care and connection. Though it may be buried beneath the facade of hostility and hidden behind the scowls of rage, it remains intact, lying in wait for the empathic connection that will coax it into the world. No matter how calcified our exterior shells may become, assaulted by the cruelties of life, the pulse of humanity beats within us. It is as instinctive as a tattooed truant rocking a baby to sleep.

For most of us, the majority of persons we routinely encounter in the course of our day are not as damaged as a homicidal gang member or even a reform school candidate seething with rage and defiance. Still, in a world where heartache gives rise to all manner of aggression, we find it easy to demonize persons who disturb or offend us. We reduce them to the behaviors and distortions we find problematic. "My ex-wife is vindictive and angry," we say to anyone who will listen. "That person with the abhorrent politics is an uncompromising, dogmatic bigot." "The eighth-grader who terrorizes the classroom is nothing but a cold-blooded thug." In demonizing others, we distance ourselves from their humanity. We forget that their hearts beat with longing and pain. For all practical purposes, we assume that the pulse of their spirits has been extinguished.

Damian reminds us otherwise. All persons we encounter—even those we are tempted to write off and dehumanize—possess the capacity for care and connection. An essence of Self resides deeply within them. They too hide an unmarred face of compassion that longs for connection. This essential core of compassion finds its source in God. As long as their hearts are beating, a sacred pulse is present within them as well—sustaining life and inviting restoration into the compassionate humanity we were all created to be. Even the most tortured and barbaric, a sadistic murderer of Jews and Christians, for example, can be transformed into a poet of love. We know one. His name is Paul of Tarsus.

Other People's Behaviors as FLAGs

Third, our recognition that others' interior worlds are constructed in precisely the same way as our own helps us cultivate compassion for them. Every interior movement we encounter in others—their emotional reactions, their conversations and self-talk, their behaviors whether impulsive or deliberate—represents a cry rooted in some form of suffering aching to be soothed, some need fighting to be secured, or some form of joy longing to be celebrated. Their emotions, words, and actions are FLAGs frantically waving for attention and care. Their actions rise out of life-threatening *fears*, unsatisfied *longings*, *aching wounds* still bleeding and raw, and *gifts* and capacities that are obstructed and stifled. Their actions seem to be saying, *I hate the world and everyone in it.* But underneath the vehemence lies a deeper cry: *I feel beaten down and alone. Someone please see me.*

The coworker who chastises us for failing to follow procedures may long simply to be taken seriously after a lifetime of feeling dismissed and devalued. The loved one who withdraws behind a mask of invulnerability may be terrified of rejection while also aching to feel safe and understood. The eighth-grader who rages at anyone around may feel powerless and alone in a world where loved ones are slain right before his eyes.

Agitated emotions, cutting discourse, difficult behaviors, even acts of violence and violation depict the tragically veiled screams of people in pain, aching to be heard, held, and healed. As counterproductive as it seems, destructive behavior and extreme emotions are desperate pleas for life and connection. They bid for power, significance, safety, and affiliation; they are rooted in wounds of abandonment, oppression, helplessness, and abuse.

To be sure, sometimes these words and deeds cause destruction. Damian's cry took the form of rage and aggression. The plea of a dying gang member took the form of murder. The path of compassion in no way condones violation or minimizes the suffering violation can cause. It does, however, offer a basis for understanding that tempers the impulse to demonize and ostracize an offender. No one is born a perpetrator. Every act of violation, however grotesquely disguised, comes from suffering and pleads for healing and restoration. This insight opens a door to empathic connection. And, as Damian so powerfully demonstrated, empathic connection has the potential to soften a hardened heart and restore our capacities for caring reconnection.

————————

At the edge of the town where I live, the residential area abuts the San Gabriel Mountains, and a wilderness park fans out with a trail that loops through the foothills. For twelve years, my family's dog and I spent more days than not driving to the park and running the scenic trail. Misty, a Siberian Husky, was my gift to my son on Christmas—also the day of Justin's birth—which was the first holiday after his mom and I split up. Justin took to Misty like a motherless child to a sibling. And, boy, did Misty love to run. When I let her off leash, a quarter mile into the trail, she would dart up the ridge in seconds, chase and scatter the birds, and tear out across a field with such an effortless glide that she looked like poetry in motion. The radiance of her running with abandon offered solace through years of life as a single parent.

The spring of Justin's first year of college, Misty fell ill. Cancer spread throughout her body, and she couldn't climb steps, let alone run the trail. Justin flew home for spring break. We took her to the vet and stroked her on the doctor's table as the recognition in her eyes faded away into the vacant stare of death. We stayed with her body for a while. The doctor came and took her. Much later, he returned with a certificate and a box of her ashes.

Justin and I pondered how to honor Misty's ashes, but one thing we knew for certain: A portion of them needed to be scattered in the wilderness park on the trail she so loved to run. The following morning, a Saturday, I dressed, gathered a vial of Misty's ashes, and drove to the trail. My time was somewhat limited—later that morning Justin would fly back to his college campus. I had just enough time to run our route while pausing at places that brought her the greatest delight.

Unfortunately, I was not the only person setting out for the wilderness park that morning. Over the years, the park had become increasingly popular. Parking, however, did not keep up with the expanding demand. The tiny lot at the trailhead often filled before dawn's first light. The single access road that led there disallowed parking altogether. The only other parking option was an overflow lot at the mouth of the access road several hundred yards away from the trail.

I knew I was in trouble the moment I got to the road. The overflow lot was so full, cars were angled into the spaces between bushes, a queue forming to take spots as they opened. Without time to wait, I drove past the line and toward the trailhead on the off chance the tiny main lot would have a vacancy. It didn't. In fact, another line of cars idled in wait for the slow trickle of walkers, runners, and bicyclists to complete their laps of the trail. I did not have time to wait there with them. So I circled around and made my way back toward the overflow lot. As I drove up the road, cars were making U-turns in front of me as the drivers realized the futility of driving all the way to the trailhead. Of course, each car circling before me put me farther behind any vacancy ahead. I was stuck at the end of growing lines whichever direction I went.

Then I passed a cul de sac. The corner house adjacent to me had an open space in front. I zipped around, turned into the court, zipped around again, and pulled up in front of the house at the foot of a sign forbidding parking at night. I still had time to do this. I grabbed my water bottle, my running watch, and the vial of ashes, leaped from the car, locked it, looked up, and immediately started to backpedal. Barreling down the driveway toward me, a leaf rake in one hand and a steel rake in the other, both outstretched and menacing as if fending off a grizzly, a large man of Middle Eastern descent was screaming at me with accented aggression.

"What're you doing?! You're parking right in front of my house!"

Being the man of compassion that I am, I instinctively yelled back, "What? I'm not doing anything wrong?" I pointed to the sign. "It says so right there."

"You're right in front of my house!" he yelled louder, jabbing with his rake. "My bushes! My lawn! My property!"

"But I'm on the street!" I insisted. "I'm not touching your property! Really. It's totally legal to park here."

He scowled. He wanted to spit, cuss, and take a swing, but he thought better. "You're not going to help me, are you?" he seethed and scolded. "You're not going to help me! Fine! The hell with you! The hell with all of you!" And he turned and stormed back toward his house.

The whole encounter lasted but seconds. My heart was racing. My stomach felt sick. What just happened? Fear of assault, shame at my defensiveness, indignation at his manner, and a desperate desire to flee the scene clamored within me at once. I did not know what to do. To buy some time, I got back in my car and tried to settle myself down. I felt pulled by competing passions. Part of me wanted to leave the car there; after all, I was doing nothing wrong. But that felt mean-spirited, a violation of the person I really yearned to be. Part of me wanted to scurry away, to give in and be done with it and just find another place to park. But that felt submissive and defeating, one more sheepish acquiescence in a lifetime of cowering before bullies. Paralyzed by the distaste of either decision, I simply sat there and tried to discern what to do.

On the one hand, I did not want to defy him and just leave my car there. He was concerned for his property, rightfully so, and worried that it would be trampled. On the other hand, I did not want to simply slink away in intimidated defeat. I wanted to claim some measure of dignity. Besides, I felt bad about how I had reacted. I wanted to prove to myself that I could respond with respect for both him and myself.

So I decided to try again. I gathered my courage, walked up to his door, and rang the bell. He answered, surprised that I was there and on guard for what I might want.

"Sir," I said. "I am really sorry. I just reacted a few minutes ago, and I did not hear what you were saying. I can see that it really bothers you to have cars parked so close to your yard. People can be careless; I'm sure it's frustrating. I'm happy to move mine. I just wanted you to know that I get it, and I'm sorry for not hearing it before."

He eyed me, still skeptical. "People park here all the time," he reinforced. "They don't care, but it's somebody's home. People live here."

"I know," I said. "I'm sorry I didn't realize it before. I was just in a hurry. My dog died, my son's dog, really. She loved that trail. I just wanted to scatter some of her ashes, then get back to my boy."

He eyed me some more, something softening. "Your dog," he said, "your boy's dog—she died, huh?" I nodded. "Yeah. My girl had a dog too. It was killed in the fighting." He looked off as if returning to some faraway land. Then he continued, softer still. "You know why I hate the people parking their cars in front of my house?" I didn't. He let out a sigh. "We're from Iraq. Baghdad." He shook his head. "Sometimes the people, they parked their cars in front of our apartment. One day, one of the cars explodes. Right in front of our house. Not twenty minutes before, my girl—my six-year-old— is playing on that street. We come to America. Now she can't sleep. Each morning, she looks out, cars parked in front of our house even here. She begs me to make the cars go away, but what can I do? Tell me, what is a father to do?"

I looked at him. His aggression had dissipated. My defensiveness had too. I had no answers. A child's terror silenced our disagreement. The parking of my car no longer mattered. However, our meeting on the porch did— two dads, bearing the sorrow of their children, seeking refuge in a world of violence and loss.

Extreme behavior, even assaults of aggression, are but the cry of some suffering aching to be heard and tended. Meeting others at the source of their pain can relax their reactivity and still their pounding heart. Moreover, it can open a space for genuine connection. That space creates holy ground, a place where we turn our swords of hostility into the plowshares of compassion for our common human plight.

Cultivating the PULSE of Compassion toward Others

Grounded in these insights, the Compassion Practice offers a way to cultivate genuine compassion for others. We must remember that we only cultivate such compassion when we feel open to connecting with another person. If we encounter someone and feel anything but compassion toward him or her, we ground ourselves, take a U-turn, and tend to the stirrings within us until our erratic pulse is steady once more. When I react with fury at my son's tardiness in picking me up, I do not force a compassionate understanding toward him and his behavior. Instead, I turn inward, recognize my own hidden insecurities, and, through the PULSE of Self-compassion, settle once more in my caring and connected core. Only then do I turn my attention toward the person before me.

As I consider Justin and his tardiness, I come face-to-face with the speck that is still lodged within his eye—he remains late and his behavior does not inspire in me a spontaneous affection for him. How do I cultivate a compassionate connection with my son when it is not immediately forthcoming? I do so in precisely the same way I cultivated compassion for myself. I connect with the PULSE of his humanity—the bid for life that beats within him and the suffering he experiences when that life is obstructed. This pulse beats, however dimly or buried, beneath the surface of any presenting emotion or behavior. Connecting with it compassionately can be done as follows.

First, we *pay attention*. We simply notice nonreactively and nonjudgmentally what others are doing and what they look like while they are doing it. We gaze upon them contemplatively, the way an artist would observe them or as if they were a character on stage or in a film. In the same way we cultivate a radical acceptance of our own interior movements, we nurture a welcoming posture and expansive hospitality toward the people we are beholding. This is how Jesus gazes upon people. For example, when he beholds the woman caught in adultery, Jesus intuits without condemnation the suffering underneath her behavior. (See John 8:1-11.) When Zacchaeus, the tax collector, calls to Jesus from a tree, Jesus recognizes the humanity that belies his pariah of a profession. (See Luke 19:1-10.) When a hemorrhaging woman, emboldened by her years of suffering, simply touches Jesus' cloak, he stops and sees her, and he offers her healing. (See Mark 5:25-34.)

By simply pausing to see others in their own unique particularity, we are paying attention. With an open, nonreactive curiosity, we take a long, loving look at the reality of their experience. Trusting that everything they do or feel has a reason and makes sense given the past they have known, we notice *their behaviors* (What are they doing, and what do they look like as they are doing it?), *their emotions* (What feelings are they experiencing, and how intensely are they feeling them?), *their words* (What are they saying, either internally or aloud, to us, to others, and to themselves?), and *their bodily expressions* (What do their bodies look like? What are the expressions on their faces? What are their postures and gestures? Do we notice any symptoms of stress or pain?) In short, we attempt to see them in the truth of their experience.

As I attempt to see Justin in the truth of his experience, I might notice that he pulls up at ten after six with a lovely smile on his face as if savoring something truly delicious. Or he might exhibit a look of dread at how late he is or an unhurried oblivion to the time at all. If I find myself reacting, I take a momentary U-turn, understanding that the log is edging back into my eye, and it needs to be heard and tended. Then I return my gaze to Justin and simply behold how he is present in the moment.

After taking the time to see others in the truth of their experience, we try to *understand empathically* the suffering underneath their actions or emotions. Their behavior, however distorted, is a bid for life or connection. Their emotions and impulses are cries. Something on which their very life depends is threatened or at stake. We cultivate empathic understanding through listening deeply to others' experiences until the sources of their behavior surface. We surface this source by asking ourselves, *What is the waving FLAG straining to be heard within the cry of what they are doing?*

Fear. What do they seem to most deeply fear? What is at stake causing them to feel or behave in this way?

Longing. For what do they most deeply long? What essential needs for the flourishing of their lives do they seem to be straining for?

Aching wound. What pains or oppression from their past can you imagine is raw and sensitive, perhaps triggered in this moment?

Gift obstructed. What strengths and capacities buried within them seem stifled and discouraged, pleading to be claimed and nurtured?

When we hear the sources of the cries within others, something shifts inside us. We are moved. Our hearts open a bit wider. And compassion for them rises within us. What might surface as I listen deeply to the cry within Justin's behavior? Perhaps Justin is savoring the start of a secret courtship too new to share with his family. Maybe he's so terrified of my criticism that he's rushing to get me while fighting back the tears of shame stinging his eyes. Or maybe he's simply relishing his summer freedom while dreading the relentless approach of the impending school year's oppressive schedule.

Understanding the deeper cry of another's soul has the capacity to move us—no wonder Justin is a few minutes late; no wonder he has that look on his face—and it activates a *loving connection* that holds him with soothing care. Like the parent who lingers at a bedroom doorway to gaze upon a sleeping child, compassion deepens as we pause to extend grace and understanding. May my boy's first taste of love be sweet. May his shame truly yield to the light of his beauty. May his capacity to enjoy the moment be a healing balm from the demands of young adulthood.

When love is revived and allowed to flow through us, we are united with God's compassion. A whispered sense of God's presence may emerge, a presence that longs to bathe this beloved in a love both infinite and enduring. We might invite this presence to surround this person—as Jesus, Mary, a symbol of the Holy Spirit, the healing warmth of God's light. Sensing the sacredness and extending it toward the person we are beholding transforms this practice into prayer. Justin is held in the presence of God—a God that holds us both.

God's love, fused with our own, aches for healing and restoration. I hope that Justin will know the glory of being fully alive in all of his unique beauty and giftedness. As compassion deepens, so does our desire to see others *embodying new life*, and we commit our intention to nurture such life into being. What fullness is unfolding in Justin—the delights of love? The grace of knowing himself as beloved? The eyes to notice the beauty that is present and the freedom to linger in its light? Our pulses beat strongly when others' deepest desires become what we desire for them.

As it turns out, Justin shares with me later that he is in love. And his beloved starts work at six each evening. He drives her to work and drops her off to squeeze in every possible second of their limited time together. Then he rushes over to pick me up, hoping not to be too late. Connecting with the pulse of life beating within his behavior has the capacity to free and deepen my compassion for him. Of course I want him to savor every minute with his new love. Taking my PULSE connects me to my compassionate core. Taking Justin's PULSE connects us to each other. Then compassion may flow freely once more.

Loving Our Enemies

Accessing our compassion and generous goodwill for a nineteen-year-old savoring the sweetness of first love or an elderly dancer now bound in a wheelchair requires only minimal work for most of us. What about people who are far more difficult? How do we cultivate compassion for those who truly threaten or repulse us? This represents the radical challenge of Jesus' spiritual path. "You have heard that it was said, 'You shall love your neighbor and hate your enemy.' But I say to you, Love your enemies and pray for those who persecute you . . . For if you love those who love you, what reward do you have? Do not even the tax collectors do the same? And if you greet only your brothers and sisters, what more are you doing than others? Do not even the Gentiles do the same?" (Matt. 5:43-44, 46-47).

Jesus' call is radical indeed. Jesus invites us to cultivate a genuine compassion even for those who offend and infuriate us. In a world where violence, mean-spiritedness, aggression, and defiance ravage our cities and homelands, permeate our political discourse, and bleed into our schools, families, and places of work, offering compassion to our enemies may be the most pressing social challenge of our day. The future of our planet, communities, and interpersonal relationships depends on finding grounded, nonreactive, nonescalating ways of responding to others when we feel threatened or diminished. The future of our soul depends on it too. For learning to love our enemies leads us down a spiritual path toward healing, vitality, and personal transformation.

We find the clue for cultivating such radical compassion in what constitutes a person as our enemy. Our enemies are people who repel us—literally. The word *enemy* comes from the Latin union of *in* (meaning "not") and *amicus* (meaning "friend" and linked to *amare*, meaning "love"). Loved ones are people to whom we feel attracted and with whom we want to connect. Enemies are people we anti-love, so to speak. They are people from whom we recoil. Connection with them feels abhorrent. Like two positively charged magnets defying contact, we resist proximity to our enemies. Emotionally, we push them away, or we pull ourselves away in aversion. This repelling energy can take many forms: rage, disgust, contempt, terror, mockery, or apathy. For us, such people restrict our impulse of compassion. We all have such people in our lives. Every day we encounter the following types of people:

People whose political or ideological views are repugnant to us—proponents of pro-choice, pro-life, immigration reform, or stronger borders;

People within certain social positions of which we are inherently suspicious—the poor, the wealthy, the military, the incarcerated;

People in the news or in our communities whose deeds particularly disgust us—acts of abuse, embezzlement, debauchery, infidelity;

People we encounter throughout the day who simply push our buttons—reckless drivers, inconsiderate neighbors, people who text while we are talking to them;

Even our friends, family, companions, and coworkers can be our "enemies" for a moment when they act in ways that trigger our fury or displeasure.

While we all have such enemies in our lives, we recognize that we do not have the same ones. The telemarketer who incites my wrath prompts another's patient politeness, while the welfare recipient who infuriates that person stirs yet another's kind regard. In fact, the very same people who trigger us one day can evoke our understanding the next. While we are tempted to insist that another's offensive behavior is inherently repulsive and defies all capacity to be met with compassion, we know the truth to be otherwise. Compassion toward this person is possible; yet, we obstruct it. The source of our repulsion lies within us. Something within us has conspired to knock us off the ground of our core and caring Self. The obstruction within us is some part of ourselves crying for care, and it is fighting to get our attention.

People who repel us are not arbitrary. They fit a profile that is unique to each of us. Only particular types of people ignite a heightened charge of reactivity within me—certain character traits, behaviors, or expressions on people's faces. For each of us, our enemies are custom-made. The reason for this is counterintuitive. People by whom we are repelled activate some part of ourselves that we have repressed—a part of ourselves we refuse to acknowledge since we are preoccupied by the person repelling us. Our reactivity is the cry of something within us that is screaming to be noticed. When we ignore that cry—when we internally repel it—our repulsion toward the other intensifies.

In short, our enemies serve as mirrors. They reflect to us that which we have relegated to the shadows of our own inner world. Our resistance to holding them with compassion is rooted in a resistance to holding ourselves with compassion. That which we find untouchable in them is tethered to something we find untouchable within us. These parts within us, consigned to the shadows, are usually one of the following:

An unhealed wound. Parts of us still carry the pain of having been wounded in precisely the same way we see our enemies bringing pain to the world.

A secret shame. Parts of us are capable of precisely the same behaviors we reject in our enemies, and we fear that if these parts are revealed, we will be rendered equally untouchable.

A threatened life-need. Parts of us that need to flourish in life or love—a need to feel safe, to be seen, to have value, or to feel included— feel threatened or jeopardized.

An undeveloped gift or power. Capacities within us—our personal power, voices, strengths, and talents—have been chronically stifled by persons our enemies represent.

These buried parts of us long to see the light of day. Unhealed wounds ache to be acknowledged and held. Secret shames ache to know compassion and forgiveness. Essential life-needs ache to be satisfied. Stifled gifts ache to be claimed and to flourish. As long as we repel these parts of ourselves from within, they will seek alternative ways to get our attention. By causing our repulsion toward others, they are screaming for care. When others repel us, compassion invites us to refrain from attacking or villainizing our enemies or even shunning them in disgusted aversion. Instead, compassion invites us to turn inward—to hear the cry within us, tend its needs, heal its wounds, and nurture its vitality. In so doing, we return to the Self-compassion that relaxes the reactivity within us and restores the pulse of our humanity. Over the course of the process, our enemies will be transformed. We will recognize them as human. They are people in pain just as we are. And the tether of our repulsion softens into the bond of compassionate connection.

An Enemy Transformed on the Softball Field

I love to play softball. I love to catch fly balls, swing the bat, and run the bases. I play the game just for the joy of it; in fact, I don't even like to keep score. I don't care who wins. I don't have a competitive bone in my body.

In other words, I am nothing like my teammate Matt.

Matt is a hothead. He slams into the catcher even if he can avoid it. He berates us—his teammates—when we make errors. He taunts opponents when they lose, and he argues with the umpires even if he's out by a mile. Quite frankly, I despise guys like Matt. He ruins the game. He's a bully. He's an embarrassment to our team. Of one thing I am certain: I could never be like him.

One day, an opposing team was one player short. I was afraid they would have to forfeit, and we would all have to go home. So I offered to play for the other team. After all, I didn't care who won. Besides, I still got to play left field.

The game was an epic battle between two equally matched teams. We led by three runs; they caught up. They led by two runs; we caught up. Another rally, another lead change. Back and forth it went until we were ahead by two in the final inning. But Matt's team tied it up in the bottom half, putting us into extra innings. We were all getting into the game, even the crowd. Players from adjacent fields, their games long since over, stood around and cheered as the marathon game continued. We scored twice in the tenth, and Matt's team tied it up. Three more runs for us in the eleventh. Three more runs tie it up for Matt. Every lead was matched taking us to thirteen innings, fourteen innings, all the way to the fifteenth inning. We scored one more run, and then Matt's team came to bat. With one out, Matt was on third base, another runner was on second, and I was out in left field.

And I knew *exactly* how Matt was going to play this. Any ball hit to the outfield for the second out, he was going to tag up and bolt for home bowling through anybody in his path to score the tying run. *Well, not on my watch!*, I thought. For once, I was going to put this guy in his place. I positioned myself an extra step back so as to make a running catch with the momentum to throw Matt out at the plate. Sure enough, a soft line drive was hit to left field. I lined it up in my sight. Matt was prepped at third. The catcher was shaking at home. I could just see it all happening. I was going to make a running catch and throw the ball to home plate. And Matt would be out.

The ball came. I lunged to catch it. I took a step, grabbed the ball, and heaved it to home plate. But wait. Something was wrong. The ball was not in my mitt. It was not at my feet. It was not anywhere in front of me. I turned around and looked behind me. In my haste, I had run right past the ball. I watched it bounding out toward the parking lot beyond the field as Matt not only scored the tying run from third but the runner on second scored the winning run as well. And I—the meek and noncompetitive guy who does not care who wins—took my mitt, threw it to the ground, and verbally berated myself.

"How could you be so stupid?" I seethed. "In front of God and everybody, you made a complete ass of yourself!" I stomped and kicked with such agitation I could not settle down to walk through the congratulatory handshake line. I stormed to my car and fumed all the way home.

Once home, I realized that I had to teach a class on compassion first thing the following morning. Without a better idea, I decided to try the Compassion Practice. So I caught my breath and got grounded. I took the U-turn instead of seething at Matt. Shame burned within me. I could just see myself standing in left field, throwing a tantrum, and storming around. I watched that man. Then something happened. The man I saw started swelling up like a balloon. It was weird. The rage and venom within him was too much for his body to contain. So he began expanding—an overinflated doll with my likeness getting bigger and bigger, a balloon like those that fly in the Macy's Thanksgiving Day Parade. He kept expanding until finally he just exploded. Balloon fragments blew all over the field. And all that was left, like the man behind the curtain in *The Wizard of Oz*, was a runty, seven-year-old boy. It was me when I was a kid in Little League, relegated to right field because I was so bad, praying to God that nobody hit the ball to me because I couldn't stand the shame of dropping it in front of everyone. And the little boy looked up at the adult me and simply said, "Why do you hate me so much?"

I realized he was right. I cannot stand people who belittle others for not being able to play well. I cannot stand them because I am just like them. I don't do it to others; I do it to myself. I hated the boy within me who had a hard time just catching the ball and ached for someone to understand his humiliation. Restored to my right mind, I could look at my younger self with compassion. I could let him know that I see him. And he no longer has to worry. In my eyes, he's a star—no matter how many balls he drops.

Then something else dawned on me. Matt harbored a little boy as well. I turned my gaze toward him. My shame had long since dissipated. So had my disgust. I could see Matt more clearly, pumping his fist in exhilaration after the win. But his eyes betrayed something else. His aggression on the field was his cry. Would anyone see the right fielder in him and understand just how humiliated he feels?

———————

The people who repel us serve as our mirrors. They reflect the buried parts of ourselves that cry out for healing and wholeness. Matt brings out of me a self-berating rage that taunts my own failure as severely as any bully on a ball field. And deeper still, I find a banished boy whose shame aches for care and compassion. These shadowed parts of me long for the light of day. So they project themselves onto people in my world who embody and rebound the repelling energy back at me. If I persist in ignoring these interior cries, they only scream louder. My repulsions toward others intensify. And sometimes these cries break through altogether in outbursts of rage and self-loathing that catch me off guard.

The secret to genuinely loving our enemies is to work with—not against—the momentum of our souls. Trying to compel compassion for Matt when he personifies those qualities I despise in myself is like biking into a one hundred-mile-per-hour headwind that only gets stronger as I keep pedaling into it. Taking the U-turn, I can ride the tailwind that takes me back home to my Self. Once there, I find the wounded boy longing for arms that will receive him. From my compassionate core, I can welcome him and soothe his terror. He is loved. And he needs nothing from any ball field to prove it. As I settle deeply into the pulse of my loving humanity, I might turn my gaze from the young boy to someone else. With eyes starving for love as well, the wounded boy in Matt stares at me. And within my compassionate core, he too is welcome.

In this way, our enemies become our spiritual teachers. They serve as allies on the road to life and love. They have the unique capacity to surface within us what most immediately longs for healing and wholeness. And in pointing us back to our Self, they lead us to the source of compassion—a compassion wide enough to hold all the world's wounded. Our enemies can be our guides. They are the faces of God in disguise.

CULTIVATING COMPASSION
FOR ANOTHER

Hearing the Cry of a Beloved or Friendly Other

1. Choose a loved one, friend, or acquaintance for whom you have some affection to be the focus for this exercise. Imagine that person involved in a behavior or experiencing an impulse or emotion that feels difficult for him or her.

2. Take his or her PULSE and cultivate a deeper understanding of what he or she might be experiencing by answering the FLAG questions. You may need to use your imagination and speculate at points.

   (Note: If you find yourself reactive or activated in any way whatsoever, recognize your feelings and invite the activated emotion, judgment, or impulse within you to relax so you can observe and reflect on this person.)

   Paying attention. Describe nonjudgmentally what you see about this friend or loved one as you observe him or her experiencing the difficult feeling, impulse, or behavior.

   > What is his or her appearance—clothes, hair, expression?

   > What is his or her behavior?

   > What does he or she seem to be feeling?

   > What else might he or she be experiencing in this situation?

   > What else might be going on in his or her life that contributes to what is happening?

Understanding empathically. Using your imagination if necessary, sense what may be the deeper suffering underneath his or her behavior using the FLAG technique.

> What might be his or her deepest *fears*?

> What might he or she most deeply be *longing* for?

> What persistent and *aching wounds* may he or she be carrying that could exacerbate the pain of the situation?

> What *gifts* might he or she possess that are being frustrated or denied at this time?

3. Summarize your sense of his or her experience by completing the sentences below. If his or her behavior were a cry of suffering, it would say the following:

> "Please understand . . . "

> "I ache for . . . "

> "Right now I most need . . . "

4. Write a prayer to a significant sacred presence in his or her life, a prayer that expresses what he or she would most deeply want the sacred to know about his or her pain, longings, or deepest needs. (If he or she is not religious, write it as a letter to someone, either living or dead, who provides a healing and sacred presence in his or her life.) Write the prayer or letter in the first person from his or her perspective.

CULTIVATING COMPASSION
FOR ANOTHER

The Compassion Practice with a Difficult Other

1. ***Catch your breath.*** Ground yourself in a way that works for you: listen to music, read a sacred text, light a candle, or sit in silence. Take several deep breaths, and ease into an interior space that feels safe, grounding, and perhaps sacred.

2. ***Take your PULSE.***

   Paying attention. Allow into your awareness various persons for whom you have difficulty feeling compassion—persons whose behavior or attitudes have triggered some form of reactivity within you recently. Of the various persons who have come to you, allow one to be the focus for this practice.

   For a moment, imagine that person and his or her behavior you find difficult. In your imagination, ask that person to recede into some sequestered room, away over the horizon, or into the light of the sacred so you can feel safe from his or her presence and influence.

   Turn your attention inward, and notice the feeling, impulse, or internal movement this person activated within you. Don't allow it to take you into its power, but don't judge or suppress it either. Simply cultivate a nonjudgmental awareness of the movement present within you. You might do this by saying to yourself, *Anger is here. I see you, anger.* Or you might notice its presence in your body and say to yourself, *I feel a tightness in my chest. I see you, tightness.*

If you feel open to understanding this movement more deeply, proceed. If not, notice what you are feeling instead, and invite that feeling to relax.

Understanding empathically. Invite this interior movement to surface the threatened need, sensitive wound, secret shame, or stifled gift underlying the movement's intensity. You may want to invite it to express itself as a person (a child, an angel, an older adult) or an object (a hot iron, a hammer). Ask this interior part of you whichever FLAG questions allow a deeper understanding and compassion within you.

> What is your deepest *fear*?

> What is your deepest *longing*?

> What *aching wound* still bleeds within you?

> What hidden *gift* feels stifled and frustrated?

Loving with connection. Let yourself feel a sense of compassionate connection to whatever part of you surfaces from within. Care for this part of you just as you would a wounded or frightened child.

Sensing the sacredness. Invite an expansive sense of sacredness—Jesus, Mary, a symbol of the Holy Spirit, the warmth of God's light—to be with this part of you in healing and life-giving ways.

Embodying new life. Notice any new life or perspective that emerges within you, and allow this gift to flow throughout your body and into every part of your being.

3. *Take the other's PULSE.*

Paying attention. Remember this person at a time when he or she was involved in the behavior that felt offensive. For a few moments, observe what he or she is doing and the particular way he or she is doing it without judgment or reactivity. Watch with an open curiosity like an artist preparing to paint a subject.

> What does the person look like—attire, facial expression, body posture?

> How does the person behave? What does he or she say? What emotions does he or she feel?

(Note: If you become activated, invite that reaction within you to relax—you are simply paying attention to this person.)

Understanding empathically. Remember that this person's words and actions are rooted in some suffering—his or her behavior is a cry aching to be heard and tended. Cultivate a deeper understanding of the suffering hidden underneath his or her behavior by engaging the FLAG questions:

> What seems to be his or her deepest *fear*?

> What seems to be his or her deepest *longing*?

> What *aching wound* seems to be stinging him or her right now?

> What *gift* seems to be frustrated and is fighting to be recognized?

Loving with connection. Allow yourself to feel a sense of compassionate connection with the suffering underneath the person's behavior just as you would with a wounded or frightened child who needs care. Extend that compassion toward the other person.

Sensing the sacredness. If it feels right, notice if an expansive sense of God is near and invite that presence—as Jesus, Mary, a symbol of the Holy Spirit, the warmth of God's light—to be with this person at the source of his or her suffering, tending him or her in whatever way feels healing and restorative.

Embodying new life. Sense the new life that yearns to be birthed within him or her, and extend your desire for this healing to flourish.

4. *Decide what to do.* Listen for an invitation of one concrete action that stays true to what you have experienced in the practice, and act accordingly when you encounter this person again. This might mean discerning ways to claim what you need for life, power, dignity, and wholeness. Or it might mean discerning ways to embody compassion for the other by remembering an image of this person in his or her suffering, carrying

a symbol of your intention to react from a caring space, or thinking of a word or phrase that helps you remember this person as a beloved and sacred human being.

In the Moment

Before you encounter this person again, take a few moments and imagine different actions, practices, or gestures that can help you stay grounded in your core when you are with him or her, especially when he or she behaves in ways that knock you off-center. Such actions might include the following:

> taking deep breaths

> visualizing your sacred space or a sacred image

> touching a symbol or object kept in your pocket

> glancing away and connecting with something in nature

> imagining light surrounding you and/or the other person

> touching your heart

> connecting with your body

> repeating a silent mantra to yourself such as *I am beloved*

> silently remembering the Serenity Prayer or the Jesus Prayer

> squeezing your index finger

> curling your toes

Experiment with these grounding actions for a few weeks. Whenever you are with this difficult person (or any other difficult person), practice actions like these, and notice what helps you stay grounded during such encounters. If you feel led, you may try to listen for the cry that is hidden underneath the person's words and behavior. Try to remember his or her suffering and humanity. Notice how you feel when you remain grounded and connected to another's humanity.

Chapter 5

Deciding What to Do

Discerning Compassionate Action

On a Friday morning in November of 2013, villainy descended upon San Francisco. A damsel in distress was tied to a bomb on the tracks of an approaching cable car. The evil mastermind who plotted the diversion was robbing a bank downtown. Lou Seal, the beloved Giants baseball mascot, was kidnapped and caged at AT&T Park. The city, held hostage to rampage and terror, was in dire need of a hero.

One came from a most unlikely place.

Five-year-old Miles Scott lives in Tulelake, California—a small farm town near the Oregon border and hundreds of miles from any metropolis. Miles was too young to know much about villainy. Or at least he should have been. As an infant, Miles suffered from constant fatigue, spikes of fever, chronic bone pain, bruising, and absence of appetite. At eighteen months, doctors diagnosed him with acute lymphoblastic leukemia, a rare form of blood cancer that could be fatal within weeks if left untreated.

For the next few years, Miles's childhood was all but stolen. While other children battled phantom foes and rival siblings, Miles fought cancer. With his father, a hay farmer, and his mother, a young farmwife, holding vigil beside him, he occupied hospital beds far from home in the distant cities of Medford and Portland. His early years were consumed by long stays in intensive care, course after course of radiation treatments, perpetual bouts with nausea and fatigue, an endless stream of needles, lab tests, toxic drugs, blood cell counts, and long stretches where the only food he could absorb came through an IV in his arm.

Miles did, however, have a healing refuge. He loved to watch *Batman* on TV with his dad. For hours on end, with Miles too weak to lift his head off the pillow, the two of them escaped into Gotham City through reruns of the original Adam West series. Because of his love of Batman, a cape became Miles's standard attire. In the hospital, at cancer treatment facilities, and during his brief respites at home, Miles dressed up as the Caped Crusader. No villain was too evil for him to take down; as Batman, death itself could be faced and defied. The superhero was so at one with Miles's identity that when asked his deepest wish, Miles said he wanted to be Batman for real, for a day.

So the Make-A-Wish Foundation decided to make it happen. The organization, dedicated to sustaining the spirits of children fighting life-threatening illness, made a deal with Miles. Through the dark days of chemotherapy and radiation and the endless nights of their gruesome side effects, Miles would hold onto his dream like a lifeline. And when his treatment was completed, he would get his wish. He would go to San Francisco, stay in a high-rise hotel, and be Batman for real, for a day.

Miles had no idea what awaited him.

By the time Miles and his family trekked to the city, they were primed for a celebration. Only a couple of months after his final treatment, the chemo port in his chest now removed, the five-year-old Miles was officially in remission. After taking on leukemia and winning, he was ready for other less ravaging opponents. As far as he knew, however, he was only coming to the city to get properly outfitted. All that he was told at the outset of the trip was that the Make-A-Wish Foundation wanted to present him with his very own custom-made Batkid suit. No Halloween costume and cape anymore; Miles would have a suit so real and life-like that he would refuse to take if off—even at bedtime. He received it Thursday evening. It fit him and his bed perfectly.

Friday morning, as directed, Miles's dad turned on the TV. The local news, an accomplice to Make-A-Wish's scheme, declared a citywide alert. Mayhem was brewing in Gotham. Commissioner Gordon—the real-life Chief of Police, Greg Suhr—came onto the screen with an emergency plea: "Batman, we need you . . . and please bring Batkid."

Miles's dad turned to him in amazement and said, "Miles, that's you!"

They rushed to the hotel lobby, Miles already fully attired. A black Lamborghini, decaled and accessorized as an authentic Batmobile, pulled up. Batman, decked out in an adult-sized version of the same suit Miles was wearing, leaped out and said, "Batkid, they need us." Miles hopped in. Flanked by a police escort worthy of a dignitary—lights flashing, motorcycles in formation—they made for Nob Hill. Reports had come in—a damsel was in distress.

Sure enough, a woman was tied to a bomb on railroad tracks with a clanging cable car on the horizon. Hundreds of onlookers flocking the streets were chanting, "Batkid, Batkid." Miles got out of the car and looked around, a bit overwhelmed. But Batman reminded him a woman was in peril; she needed Batkid. The pint-sized superhero rose to the challenge. He clenched his fists, tightened his lips, and rushed toward the danger with great determination. He pulled the wires to deactivate the bomb and untied the terrified woman. The crowd cheered, the cable car stopped, and the woman knelt down and embraced her rescuer. Batkid had saved her. Miles patted her shoulder, still taken aback by all that he had just witnessed.

Unfortunately, there was no time to rest. The Riddler had been spotted sneaking into a bank in the financial district. Jumping back into the Batmobile, the Dynamic Duo raced downtown. Another chanting crowd awaited with posters boasting *Batkid Rocks* and *I Believe in Batkid*. As they pulled up, Batkid rushed into the bank, spied the culprit, and trapped the Riddler inside a locked vault. The police came, cuffed the bandit, and emerged from the bank with the victorious hero to display the villain now in custody. The crowd cheered—and it was growing. Even passersby were stopping to see what was happening.

Buoyed by the joyous commotion, the heroes took a break for burgers and milkshakes in Union Square. The crowd followed like fans would celebrities. A crowd numbering in the thousands filled the plaza; people climbed trees and shimmied up lampposts to catch a glimpse of Batkid in the café. Impromptu signs pervaded the throng—*Batkid Is Our Hope*, *You're Our Hero*, and *SF Loves Batkid*. In front of the restaurant, a flash mob erupted dancing to the Journey song "Don't Stop Believin'." The entire crowd sang along. A spontaneous festival erupted right in the heart of the city.

But wait. The Penguin had kidnapped the Giants mascot. As one, the crowd chanted, "We need Batkid. We need Batkid." Batkid, growing more confident in his powers by the minute, flashed a thumbs-up from the restaurant window. He was on it. Back at the Batmobile, Miles and Batman raced to AT&T Park where they frantically searched for the captive mascot.

Batkid freed Lou Seal from a cage and spotted the Penguin trying to escape. A wild chase ensued throughout the ballpark until Batkid tackled the Penguin on the field. The media took pictures. Batkid saved the day once more, and the city decided to show its gratitude.

In front of the ballpark, a police motorcade arrived with sirens and fanfare worthy of a World Series championship parade. Navigating through cheering crowds now six deep on the sidewalk, the Batmobile headed toward City Hall. A crowd of some twenty thousand people had gathered—many of them recruited volunteers, many more onlookers caught up in the excitement. The San Francisco mayor, a US Justice department attorney, the Chief of Police, the editor of the city paper, and the Regional Director of the FBI were waiting for Batkid to arrive. The mayor gave Batkid a key to the city and deputized him as a federal agent. The *San Francisco Chronicle* unveiled a special edition of the next day's paper with the headline "Batkid Saves City." And in response to the raucous cheers, Miles raised his arms in triumph and unmasked himself for all to see. Miles from Tulelake was Batkid. Miles from Tulelake was the fearless victor over villainous foes.

People from across the world were moved by Miles's story. Facebook posts and Twitter images from Italy, the United Kingdom, Australia, and Korea celebrated Batkid. Even Washington, D.C., appreciated the depths of Batkid's heroism. President Obama sent a video from the White House in which he summed up the sentiments of those around the world. "Way to go, Miles!" he declared from the Oval Office. "Way to save Gotham."

Yes. Way to go, Miles. And while we are at it, way to go, Gotham. Way to replenish the spirit in a child. Way to replenish ours as well.

The Restorative Power of Compassionate Action

For a five-year-old boy battling leukemia, San Francisco is a city, as the chief of police later observed, "with its heart in the right place"—a heart that beats to the pulse of compassion. The people were touched by the tenacity of a child with cancer who fought and defeated the illness that would take him. They understood his longing for superhero powers to take on the forces that threaten life. And they celebrated those powers being claimed—in Miles's pint-sized earnestness, his revelry in the fantasy, his fist pumps of victory, and the joy of his childhood dream fulfilled.

This abundance of compassion went far beyond sentiment. It began there—with people moved by a boy's pain and longing—but it did not end there. It incarnated such sentiment into concrete acts of kindness, care, encouragement, and restoration. These acts proliferated throughout the city—designers crafted costumes, car dealers loaned Lamborghinis, inventors constructed elaborate props, flash mob organizers choreographed dance moves, newspapers printed special editions, public officials made media appearances, thousands drove in from around the city to decorate placards and populate the chanting crowds. Compassion begs for embodiment. Without action, compassion becomes sentimentality. Embodied compassion touches the soul of another and galvanizes a city along the way.

As exemplified in San Francisco, acts of compassion restore us. To be sure, they buoy the spirits of those who are suffering. Caring presence beside the bedridden, casseroles left on a doorstep, notes of encouragement found in the mailbox, a wordless embrace when a loved one has passed—acts of care and kindness can stoke the embers of the human spirit when affliction threatens to dim them. Embodied compassion on Batkid Day helped a five-year-old cancer survivor come to discover the superhero powers already within him. He is the boy, after all, who can take on the forces that threaten life. His outstretched arms and beaming smile on a dais in front of City Hall were evidence enough. Through a city's extravagant kindness, Miles Scott's wish came true—he was Batman for real and for more than a day.

Acts of compassion also restore the people moved to embody them. Extending kindness feels good. Taking time to care for another replenishes the pulse of our spirits as well. It frees us from the impulses that deaden and disconnect us. It grounds us once more in who we really are—the core Self that composes our truest essence. And it deepens our connection to God's Spirit of life that renews us and sustains our hope. The satisfaction on the faces of the innumerable volunteers testified to this restorative power of compassion. Many of them ditched work or school to take part. To them, it was more than worth it. Their hearts, opened to Miles's plight, expanded even further in acting on their compassion. One volunteer, having driven a hundred miles merely to be an extra in the crowd celebrating Batkid, summed it up this way: "Imagining that child in intensive care, then seeing him glow with his hands in the air, I have to be honest. I felt selfish. I'm the one leaving with hope for the future." Love resuscitates life within us.

Acts of kindness also restore those looking from the sidelines. Compassion is contagious. Seeing a person care for another can inspire care within us as well. In San Francisco, pedestrians, tourists, cab drivers, cyclists, even bankers and lawyers extending their lunch breaks, were captured by the fervor of compassion. The multitudes at City Hall—along with those around the world watching through Facebook posts, Twitter, and cell phone videos—found genuine inspiration in the heroism of a five-year-old cancer survivor and in the heroics of kindness that shouldered and celebrated him. What began as the wish of a boy fighting cancer in a rural town in California became a worldwide outpouring of kindness. This expanding circle of care renewed the spirits of all drawn into its reach. It offered a glimpse of the transcendent force that truly can transform the evils of our planet—the contagion of compassion that has the power to unite the human community.

The Dark Knight, the guardian of good in the world, would be proud.

Embodied Compassion in the World

The way of radical compassion leads to embodied acts of restorative care. Jesus teaches a spiritual path centered on love. And we embody love through concrete actions that aim to ease the pain of those who suffer and promote the flourishing of life for all. As he teaches in the parable of the final judgment where the sheep and the goats are separated, the extent to which we embody love can be seen using the following litmus test: Do we feed the hungry, satisfy the thirsty, welcome the stranger, clothe the naked, free the oppressed, and visit the sick and imprisoned? (See Matthew 25:31-46.) Indeed, embodying compassion toward those in need serves the Jesus who, out of compassion, identifies himself with the wounded of the world. For Christians, embodying love means embodying Christ. Our bodies, acting with love, gives flesh to God's compassion for the world.

True compassion is engaged. It expresses itself in tangible ways. The forms of such engagement vary. Compassionate action can be embodied through the following:

Generosity. Compassion often takes the form of offering resources to ease others' suffering. Giving money to a tsunami relief organization or to a homeless person on a curb flows from our genuine care and concern. Donations to the Make-A-Wish Foundation skyrocketed in the wake of Batkid's sojourn through San Francisco.

Service. Perhaps most commonly, compassion takes the form of caring directly for the immediate needs of those who are suffering—nursing the sick, feeding the hungry, sitting with the grief-stricken, clearing rubble after a disaster, helping the injured find medical assistance. Acts of healing, care, kindness, and presence offer material comfort and spiritual balm. Thousands of such acts—some rather simple, others quite elaborate—tended the needs and buoyed the spirits of Miles Scott and his family.

Witness. Compassion can involve bearing witness to the plight of those who suffer—vigils for peace and freedom abroad, prayer services for abused children, street corner signs in protest of the dumping of chemical waste, bumper stickers pleading to end human trafficking. In Buenos Aires, the *Madres de Plaza de Mayo*, known also as the "Mothers of the Disappeared," gathered weekly for decades in peaceful opposition to the thousands of children abducted, tortured, and buried in unmarked pits. Their presence not only solidified resistance to a brutal military regime but also emboldened other woman around the globe to stage similar protests for indignities in their homelands.

Solidarity. Compassion can take the radical form of sharing the plight of those whose suffering eludes short-term remedies—living on skid row; working alongside day laborers; moving to Zimbabwe, Haiti, or South Central Los Angeles; serving the destitute in Gaza or Calcutta. Such acts of solidarity profoundly subvert the social orders that keep us separated from those who suffer.

Empowerment. Compassion can go beyond attending to the material needs of those who suffer. Compassion can empower them with the skills, tools, and personal capacities to sustain their own survival and flourishing. Acts of empowerment recognize the subtle dependency that long-term caregivers can inadvertently encourage, and they evade the threat of paternalism that can creep unconsciously into service providers. Empowerment is the difference between bringing fish to the hungry and teaching them how to fish. It is the difference between being the superhero who saves a child's life and helping the child discover the superhero already within him. Both have their places. Both serve life. Care without empowerment breeds dependency; empowerment without care subverts the spirit.

Justice. Finally, compassion can attend to the structural causes that give rise to suffering in the first place. The pain that moves us is nestled within social conditions that perpetuate it. People ravaged by hunger, discrimination, violence, and disease live within a web of social complexities. Their affliction is rooted in and aggravated by power inequities, cultural prejudices, unjust economic systems, inattentive institutional policies, and oppressive political powers. And suffering will continue as long as the social structures that sustain it remain unchecked and untransformed. Compassionate action, therefore, can take the form of public advocacy, political lobbying, education, reform campaigns, nonviolent resistance, and civil disobedience. Compassion seeks justice. Justice is compassion politically configured.

In various ways, we can embody compassion. The sentiment of being moved by others' experiences gives rise to concrete acts of restorative care. The heart softened becomes the hand extended. We become the body of Christ in the world.

Empowered Compassion in the Midst of Violence

To be sure, we live in a wounded world. Jesus' spiritual path invites us to be instruments of God's compassion through concrete acts of care. We also live in a violent world. Perpetrators of abuse, violation, bigotry, and bloodshed ravage our families and communities. What does Jesus' way of compassion look like for those who face assaultive acts of violence or the insidious degradation from persons or systems that chronically abuse and dehumanize? Certainly, Jesus was well aware of violence. A foreign power occupies his homeland. His own leaders—brutal, corrupt, and depraved—tyrannize the poor, slaughter the innocent, and live lavishly because of a profitable alliance with the Empire. Farms are increasingly confiscated. Labor is conscripted. Taxation is backbreaking. And dissent and revolt are viciously crushed, as the beheading of John the Baptist and the massacres at Masada and Jerusalem unequivocally attest.

Within this world of indignity and violence, Jesus comes not simply as a spiritual teacher but as a social prophet as well—like Cesar Chavez, Dorothy Day, Nelson Mandela, Harriet Tubman, and other advocates of social transformation inspired by his teachings. He promotes a vision of society—the kin-dom of God—where the poor would be fed, the lowly lifted up, the oppressed liberated, the corrupt exposed. Justice would reign in the kin-dom of God, wealth and power would be shared, and relationships between all persons would be restored around principles of dignity, equality, and accountable reconciliation. This kin-dom ordered around God's character and God's values would be governed by the politics of compassion.

Jesus not only inspires the imagination with this dream for society but also teaches a means for creating it within the tyrannies of violence and injustice. We can attain this "Promised Land" of social transformation through the path of empowered, nonviolent compassion. Jesus summarizes this path in the Sermon on the Mount, offering a veritable primer on social action grounded in empowered compassion.

> "You have heard that it was said, 'An eye for an eye and a tooth for a tooth.' But I say to you, Do not resist an evildoer. But if anyone strikes you on the right cheek, turn the other also; and if anyone wants to sue you and take your coat, give your cloak as well; and if anyone forces you to go one mile, go also the second mile. . . . You have heard that it was said, 'You shall love your neighbor and hate your enemy.' But I say to you, Love your enemies and pray for those who persecute you" (Matt. 5:38-41, 43-44).[1]

Since these passages have been grossly—even dangerously—misinterpreted through the ages, we should explore them with care. What does turning the other cheek and loving our enemies look like, say, for a woman suffering from domestic violence or an abuse survivor whose perpetrator wants to see his grandchildren? How do we respond to violence with empowered compassion without condoning violation, perpetuating injustice, or endangering ourselves or others by refusing to hold perpetrators accountable? Jesus' teaching offers insight.

Instinctively, we respond to violence in one of two ways: fight or flight. Flight entails fleeing the violence and allowing it to continue unchecked. Such flight can take various forms:

> *Avoidance.* We steer clear of the violence, assert that it isn't our problem, look the other way, or deny that it really exists or is as bad as others say it is.

Acquiescence. We get used to the violence, rationalizing that it is just the way things are and believing that nothing can be done about it anyway.

Accommodation. We make the best of the violence, minimizing it by telling ourselves it could certainly be a lot worse. We are careful not to make things worse by needlessly protesting or upsetting the powers that be.

When we respond to violence with flight, we never confront or transform the oppressive person or system. The violence continues. And we are dehumanized in the process—we accept our victimization and cower in submissive passivity.

Fight responds to violence with violence—an eye for an eye, a tooth for a tooth. If someone hits us, we retaliate; we hit them back—verbally, emotionally, physically—until they stop. Originally, the Hebrew law of an "eye for an eye" was meant to limit escalating violence. In a world where the murder of a single tribesperson might give rise to the slaughter of an entire village, the law mandated that a just retaliation was limited to an equal measure—a life for a life, an eye for an eye. This logic, however, contains a flaw: Violence only escalates violence. Retaliation only inflames greater hostility and inspires further retaliation. A Russian folktale illustrates this cycle of violence.

Two merchants become bitter enemies. They spread malicious rumors about each other, they steal each other's customers, and they sabotage each other's shops until, driven by their reciprocating rage, they square off in the middle of town. One shopkeeper bares his fists at the other. The second draws a knife. The first counters with a samurai sword. The second pulls out a pistol. The first comes back with a rifle. The second whisks out a dynamite stick. The first barrels forth with a dynamite bundle and defiantly lights the fuse. Finally, an angel, grieving the depth of vengeance and alarmed at the escalating violence, intervenes. She snuffs out the fuse and then parlays with the first man on the side. She tells him that she is prepared to grant him any wish in the world—extravagant riches, abundant children, a king's palace, anything he desires at all . . . with one condition: Whatever he wishes for himself, she will grant to his rival twofold.

The shopkeeper muses over the dilemma, desiring wealth yet bitter at the prospect of his rival's double share. Finally, he knows what he wants. He turns to the angel and confirms, "Whatever I wish for, my rival will receive twofold?" The angel nods. "Then what I want for myself is one blind eye."

This folktale illustrates the flaw of fight: If someone hits us, we want to hit them back *harder*. If a terrorist attacks us, we want to obliterate the terrorist *and his or her friends*. Violence does not eliminate violence; it only breeds more violence while poisoning our own soul in the process. And at the end of the day, as Tevya from *Fiddler on the Roof* foresees, the world ends up blind and toothless.

Jesus offers a third way—the way of empowered compassion. It resists evil with the weapons of love and dignity and not with hate or submissive endurance. He illustrates what this looks like through three concise examples that New Testament scholar Walter Wink brilliantly elucidates.[2] First, Jesus invites us to turn the other cheek. Often, we understand his words as a form of naïve passivity—if someone strikes us once, we roll over and let him or her strike us again. Such a response misses the point. Telling a battered woman to submit to further assault from her abusive husband violates her safety and dignity. It also violates Jesus' teaching.

Jesus' instructions are specific: If someone strikes us on the right cheek, we should turn the other also. If someone slugs us in anger with his or her right hand, the blow would land on our left cheek. The left hand, in the Middle Eastern culture of the time, was considered unclean—a person would be fined for waving a left hand, let alone hitting someone with it. The only way to hit someone on the right cheek using the right hand is to backhand him or her. A backhanded slap does not show aggression; instead, it imparts humiliation. In a culture where honor is paramount, to strike an equal in such a degrading way carries an exorbitant fine. Clearly, Jesus describes a situation where a person in a position of power strikes an inferior with the intent of humiliating him—a master to a slave, a Roman to a Jew, a wealthy landowner to a moneyless peasant.

When so slapped, the victim, seemingly, has only two options—fight or flight. If the victim fights back, he or she will suffer severe retribution. If the victim "flees" by wordlessly accepting the attack, he or she will surrender to the indignity of the situation. Turning the other cheek is a third option, and it leads to something remarkable. When the person knocked back from being backhanded steps forward and offers the other cheek, that person stands taller, reclaims his or her center, asserts personal power, and radiates an emboldened dignity. Nonverbally, he or she is essentially saying, "Try again. Your first blow aimed to humiliate me, but I refuse to let you." This places the aggressor on the defensive. The aggressor cannot backhand the person again as that person's right cheek is now hidden behind the asser-tiveness of the posture. And to strike him or her with a fist is to acknowledge him or her as an equal, a victory in and of itself for the victim. An aggres-sor's attempt to humiliate an inferior has backfired, and his or her power to dehumanize another has evaporated altogether. Gandhi's teachings also resonate with this wisdom: "The first principle of nonviolent action is that of noncooperation with everything humiliating."[3]

Reverend James Lawson, a nonviolent activist with Martin Luther King Jr., recounts an example of such a dignified and disarming response during the Civil Rights Movement. Lawson was leaving a café in the rural south when a passing motorcyclist spat into his face and then pulled into a parking lot across the street. Lawson wiped the spit off his face with his handkerchief, walked over to the cyclist, and with dignified nonchalance, asked the cyclist for directions to a nearby town. The nonplussed motorcyclist knew of nothing else to do but give the man directions as if Lawson were his social equal.

Turning the other cheek when confronted with violence hardly represents an exercise in masochistic passivity. It is an empowered form of action that refuses to be humiliated in the face of dehumanization, claims our dignity, seizes the initiative, and invites the aggressor into an appropriate mutual rela-tionship. Such an action may be dangerous—a master may beat the insolence out of a slave who turns the other cheek; a motorcyclist may blow up in rage. But the action never offers a cowering acquiescence to an oppressive situation. It is bold. Through it, we stand up for our own humanity.

Jesus' second example also requires close examination. In what context would a person be forced to "go one mile"? What does that mean? Palestine was an occupied country. A Roman soldier could requisition a Jew for ser-vile tasks, as Simon of Cyrene experienced when forced to carry Jesus' cross on the way to Golgotha. (See Matthew 27:32; Mark 15:21; Luke 23:26.) Roman legal codes, however, placed limits on such forced labor so as not to incite unnecessary unrest. A Roman soldier, for example, while hiking between posts with a heavy pack, could force a Jew to carry the pack—but only for one mile. If the soldier exploited the situation and forced the Jew to carry the pack farther, the soldier could be punished by his superior—per-haps fined or even flogged. What happens when the Jew forced to go one mile follows Jesus' invitation and goes an extra mile? The Jew's response places the soldier on the defensive, and the soldier may even beg for his pack back so as not to get into trouble. Once more, the person victimized seizes the initiative, refuses to be humiliated, and walks with a power and a dignity that the victimizer cannot erode.

Similarly, Jesus' third example refers to a specific context. Who is sued for a coat? Only the poorest of the poor, the homeless person so mired in debt that he or she literally owns nothing but the coat on his or her back. With the accumulation of land and wealth among the urban elite, such poverty and indebtedness were rampant in Jesus' time. People were in debt without a means to repay and with nothing left to confiscate. As a token of collateral, a destitute debtor could be sued for his or her coat—his or her very last possession. However, since the coat was all that the debtor had to sleep in, Jewish law demanded that the creditor return the coat to the debtor each evening, only to confiscate it once more the following morning. (See Exodus 22:25-27; Deuteronomy 24:10-13.)

The cloak Jesus refers to served as the undergarment, the only other item of clothing the debtor would be wearing. (Boxer shorts and lingerie, of course, were not yet invented.) If the debtor, following Jesus' invitation, gave his or her cloak as well, he or she would be standing in the courtroom stark naked. Nakedness was taboo in Jewish culture, a sin. It brought shame, however, not on the person who was naked but on anyone who saw another person naked. (Noah, for example, is not cursed for sleeping naked; Ham, however, is for seeing his father's nakedness. See Genesis 9:20-27.) In addition, the naked one now stood in the tradition of the prophet Isaiah who also went naked as a symbol of protest. Once more, the victimized turns the tables, steps into personal power, seizes the initiative, exposes injustice, and refuses to participate with the forces that dehumanize. Jesus' spiritual path offers bold, creative, and empowering options in the face of violence. It does not fight back with a violence that will only escalate the hostility, nor does it passively submit to the abusiveness of the situation. It resists violence but with courage, initiative, and a backbone of dignity no oppressor can ever break.

Jesus does, however, offer a qualification. He invites us to stand up against violence, to claim our dignity, and to do so while loving the one who violates us. This is a radical invitation rooted in his spiritual commitments. He believes that God's compassion extends to all of humanity, even to those who are mired in the passions and patterns of violence; he believes that all people, no matter how tortured and twisted they may become, bear a spark of humanity that dignifies their soul; and he believes a perpetrator's behavior, however violent and violating, is rooted in suffering. No one is born a perpetrator of abuse and cruelty. Only a soul battered and beaten calcifies into the coldness that inflicts pain on another.

Seeing a perpetrator of violence with compassion helps us maintain our own humanity as we confront injustice. Standing up against violence from a spirit of defiance, disgust, and demonization may be the easy response. When we do so, however, we only mirror the ones we oppose. We fight with their weapons. We return hate with hate, contempt with contempt, dehumanization with further dehumanization. In loving our enemies, however, we stay true to the image of God within us. We rise to the dignity of our truest Self; we rob others of the power to mar the face of our emboldened and loving humanity.

We also fight back with the weapons that truly transform. People who perpetrate violence expect to be hated; they expect to be defied or fled from in fear. They do not expect to be loved. Resisting violence with the weapons of compassion has the capacity to touch the humanity in perpetrators' souls. Compassion treats others with dignity even while confronting their violence, hears others with genuine understanding even when they espouse repugnant viewpoints, invites others into right and accountable relationship even when their deeds are egregious, and grieves the suffering of dangerous people even when we are forced to detain and sequester them. For Jesus, these weapons transform hearts of stone into hearts of flesh. These weapons usher in the kin-dom of God. These weapons make guns and bombs obsolete.

Putting Empowered Compassion into Action

So what does empowered compassionate resistance to violence look like in today's world? What is Jesus' invitation, for example, to the sexual abuse survivor being pressured to make nice and attend a family function where her stepfather abuser will be present? Or to the parents whose daughter has been killed by her boyfriend in a deadly fit of rage? Or to the communities of people beaten down and oppressed simply by virtue of their race, class, religion, or sexual orientation? Acts of radical compassion can be agonizingly complex. They require spiritual preparation, creativity, determination, and careful discernment. Inspired by Jesus, warriors of compassion from around the globe have modeled how destructive people can be confronted with power, compassion, and accountability. Jesus' spiritual path illuminates four actions that truly embody the way of radical compassion to guide our responses to violence.

First, acts of radical compassion are grounded in God's love as the source of truth and power. A Christian exemplar in Zimbabwe named Mawanda exemplifies how critical this is.

Mawanda's eyes bore her weariness as much as her body. She knelt in the back of the church in prayer, and her eyes stared at the floor. Mawanda was nearing eighty years old. During most of her adult life, she lived within the brutal dictatorship that held the poor hostage in Zimbabwe. She endured it all without protest—the withering farmlands, the pilfering of goods by thugs, the rumors of torture camps run by corrupt police squads. She survived compliantly until her husband and her son were arrested in the middle of the night and driven away in hoods, never to be seen again. In response, Mawanda organized a weekly vigil each Friday afternoon at the police station. Beatings, tauntings, and public strip searches did not deter her. She mobilized those she could if not to revolt then at least to witness and to protest.

Mawanda, along with twenty other women, came to the church that Sunday morning straight from jail. She and the other women were arrested at the Friday vigil. The police kept them in jail for two days without food and released them only after a pastor intervened, promising to ask the women to suspend the vigils.

Mawanda had earned her weariness—both body and soul had been battered through months of resistance. In that moment, even if she didn't have the strength to pray, she could, at least, kneel and rest. Then music began—a mix of indigenous folk songs, Christian praise choruses, and African civil rights anthems. The congregation clapped and swayed, softly at first. But, as is customary in Zimbabwean worship, the rhythm grew stronger, the clapping became whooping, and the swaying became dancing. The music surrounded everyone within its reach, including Mawanda. Like healing oil seeping deeply into aching joints, it soothed, restored, and emboldened the entire assembly. Mawanda rose and, buoyed by the community's spirit, made her way to the pulpit. Once there, she swayed and clapped and sang until the music ran its course. Then she spoke.

"When I was in jail, one of the militia—a boy, one from our own community—asked me, 'Why do you keep this up? You are old, and you have no hope. We will beat you down until you can't get up, and the vigils will come to an end.'

"I'm telling you what I told him. I do it because the power within me is stronger than the power of this world. The world's power—all it knows is violence, fear, and degradation. It's only strength is its lies: you are nobody, you can do nothing, you're just another body to be dumped on the heap of the forsaken and forgotten.

"But I'm telling you there is a power greater than the power of this world. It is the power of the One who sides with the victimized, the power of the One who says 'I hear the cries of the oppressed, and I will raise the lowly. I will not let my children wail in pain alone.'

"We are not nobody; we are children of God. We are not powerless; we can stand up for dignity and justice. We are not just bodies to be beaten and silenced; we will rise up—out of the grave if necessary—to witness against tyranny. They can kill our body, but they cannot kill our soul. They can beat our flesh, but they cannot defeat our spirit. They can harass us, berate us, intimidate us, but they cannot rob us of the truth. The power in us does not die. It is the power of life, it is the power of freedom, and it is the power of God. And nobody can take that power from us. Nobody."

Two weeks later, after two more weeks of vigils, Mawanda disappeared from her home in the middle of the night. By noon the next day, the vigil at the police station exceeded the capacity to jail all the protesters.

So the protest sang on.

It still sings today.

Radical compassion is well rooted in the true source of our worth, our power, and our hope. Acts of violence threaten to sabotage our truth. They seek to erode our spirit with their insidious lies—we are unworthy; we deserve our violation; we are alone, powerless, and abased; the oppressor holds all the leverage over the flourishing of our lives. Grounding ourselves in God evaporates any leverage oppressors may have. No matter what they do or say or threaten, we know the truth: We belong to God. We are and ever will be God's beloved. God is the foundation to our dignity, power, and capacity for compassionate resolve. No one has the power to take that from us. As both Jesus and Mawanda show us, death itself cannot rob us of this power.

Second, acts of radical compassion in the face of violence promote and preserve the flourishing of the victim's humanity. All too often, people are counseled to extend compassion in the midst of relationships that are violating or abusive. A colleague is assaultive with demeaning behavior, and the worker is encouraged to take the high road and endure it with patient understanding. A family gathering includes a former abuser, and the adult survivor is beseeched to forgive and forget and to take part in the reunion without dampening its festivity. A spouse is violent, and the victim is advised to love the batterer and honor the sanctity of marriage by enduring the abuse in silence. These are not ideals to be lauded and emulated; they are violations of compassion and distortions of Jesus' spiritual path.

Jesus invites us to turn the other cheek—to stand up to violation with dignity, personal power, courage, and a commitment to survive, even flourish, in the face of that which would degrade us. As such, the way of radical compassion does not diminish our humanity, minimize our needs for healing and wholeness, leave us vulnerable to violation, silence us, eclipse us, or render us powerless. It acts in ways that embolden our personal power in the face of an abuser. These acts could include saying no, setting boundaries, asserting our voice, honoring our needs, claiming space, gathering solidarity, confronting abuse, reporting violations, or securing a season of healing away from the difficult situation. These are acts of empowered compassion, that is, showing compassion toward ourselves.

Miraculously, our souls reveal to us that which we need to feel safe and vital. In the same way that our bodies feel pain or fever when bruised or infected, our souls communicate with us when something threatens their well-being. The indignation we feel at a demeaning coworker, the rage at a former abuser, the fear of a violent partner, the resistance to the very notion of forgiveness or compassion—these are cries coming from within, guiding us to the springs of our well-being. Compassionate action heeds these cries and discerns ways to step toward power, dignity, and personal flourishing.

Sue Monk Kidd writes of a time when she stops into a drugstore where her fourteen-year-old daughter works after school. She pauses for a moment when she spies her daughter kneeling in the aisle, stocking a bottom shelf with toothpaste. As Kidd watches, two middle-aged men walk up the aisle and pause behind her daughter. One smirks to the other, "Now that's how I like to see a woman—on her knees." The other man just chuckles as Kidd's daughter, hearing it all, drops her head in humiliation.

As Kidd describes her experience, something pierces her to the core. She watches her daughter, crouched and disgraced, and sees in her every woman shamed into submission before brutish men. She knows if she walks away in silence, her daughter's spirit could dim, condemning her to the interior posture of always being on her knees. Kidd won't let that happen.

Kidd walks up to the two men and says, "I have something to say to you, and I want you to hear it." The men stop laughing. "This is my daughter. . . . You may like to see her and other women on their knees, but we don't belong there. *We don't belong there!*"

The two men are dumbstruck. Then one of them says snidely, "Women," and the two walk away.

The daughter stands up and smiles at her mother. Kidd smiles back. Then they part, one back to work, the other back home. That night, the daughter comes to her mother's bedroom and says, "Mama, about this afternoon in the drugstore . . . "

"Yeah?"

"I just wanted to say, thanks."[4]

This is turning the other cheek.

———————

Third, radical compassion in the face of violence recognizes the humanity and dignity of others however violent or offensive they may be. As Martin Luther King Jr. taught about nonviolence, compassion refuses to hate. It realizes that even perpetrators of violence are human beings as well. They suffer. They long. They dream. They bear a pulse of goodness within them. Radical compassion seeks to genuinely understand the pain and cry hidden within others' violent actions, offensive viewpoints, vicious rhetoric, or political oppressiveness. Without condoning their violence or relinquishing our own truth and power, radical compassion is moved by the suffering that gives rise to hardened behavior. It listens for and honors the fears and terrors that underlie extreme behaviors or ideologies. It recognizes that even the corrupt and abusive are enslaved to ideologies, systems, and structures of domination, a slavery that mars but does not obliterate the spark of humanity that dwells within their God-given core. Jesus asks us to love our enemies and treat them with dignity and care, even while resisting their violence.

In Nashville, Tennessee, civil rights leaders staged nonviolent protests to end segregation. On a Saturday afternoon, college-aged African Americans courteously but assertively filled lunch counters designated for whites only. The restaurant staff refused to serve them. So the activists sat and did their homework. The second week, the restaurants hired thugs to harass the activists. The thugs spat on them, dropped food on their heads, and hurled racial epithets in their faces. Throughout, the activists refused to respond in kind. They were taught to fight hate not with hate but with love.

The third week, the arrests began. But groups of nonviolent protesters replaced each wave of activists hauled away to jail. Still, the activists maintained their dignity and treated each party—the police, the thugs, the restaurant staff, the rabid crowds of chanting bystanders—with dignity as well. They knew that once segregation was inevitably abolished, they would have to share a city together.

Weeks of sit-ins turned into an economic boycott of the entire downtown. Revenues plummeted. The demonstrations multiplied. The home of a prominent African American attorney was bombed. Finally, Nashville's mayor consented to a public meeting. He went on record to say it was time to end segregation. It was time to live together in peace. The restaurant owners, however, had one request. Afraid of national shame and its economic fallout, they asked the civil rights leaders to refrain from making a public announcement lauding their landmark victory. The restaurants would open the counters without drawing attention to it—blacks and whites would simply begin to eat side by side. Forgoing the potential public relations bonanza, the civil rights leaders agreed. Sustaining the dignity of their fellow townspeople was deemed more important than relishing their victory in front of them—as was eating together in peace.[5]

———

Fourth, radical compassion in the face of violence invites the offender into a right and appropriate relationship. Jesus yearns for reconciliation—the estranged will be reunited, enemies will heal their differences, and perpetrators of violence will be restored to the communities that they betrayed. Radical compassion hopes for such reconciliation, and invites it even with those who act egregiously. Reconciliation, however, is neither naïve nor cavalier. Reconciliation has conditions. It requires the following:

Repentance. The violent or abusive person repents and admits the wrong he or she committed.

Remorse. He or she shows remorse for the pain his or her actions caused.

Restitution. He or she makes restitution, if only symbolically, in an attempt to restore that which was lost.

Rehabilitation. He or she commits to take steps toward his or her recovery so that further violation no longer occurs.

Compassion connects empathically. It invites an offender to return to his or her own humanity. Compassion, however, is not reconciliation. It extends the hand of restoration, but the offender must reach back with a repentant hand of his or her own.

In Tallahassee, Florida, the parents of a teen killed by her boyfriend embodied such radical compassion. They invited the young man into a process of healing and redemption. They gathered with a mediator, a judge, the young man's parents, and a table full of their daughter's heirlooms huddled around her picture. The parents, without minimizing their pain, shared their unfathomable grief. The young man, without self-justification, shared his heartbroken remorse and filled in the details of the murder, answering each question from the parents. Together they agreed to a plan for rehabilitation that included time served, anger management training, and a domestic violence recovery program. The boyfriend pledged to make symbolic amends— to work in an animal rescue shelter in homage to the young woman's love for animals and to found an organization devoted to public awareness about the prevalence of teen dating violence.[6]

The restorative justice and the tough-love compassion of two extraordinary parents restored a young man's humanity. The parents demonstrated that compassionate action can recognize an offender's suffering without minimizing the pain that the offender caused. It can affirm the dignity of someone who has perpetrated a violation while holding him or her responsible for the consequences of his actions. And it can honor our own needs for healing while inviting the violator into an appropriate, accountable relationship.

———————

These warriors of compassion embody Jesus' radical spiritual path. In summary, they stay grounded in God as the source of their truth and power, they promote and preserve the flourishing of the victim's humanity, they recognize the humanity and dignity of others, and they invite offenders into right and accountable relationship. Without sentimentality, they confront brutality and abuse. They do so with the hope that even the hardened hearts of the violent will beat once more with the pulse of restored humanity.

Tragically, some hearts will remain hard. Perpetrators may remain defiant. Ideologues may prove inflexible. Systems of oppression may not yield. At such times, compassion can be moved by the traumas and terrors that breed such calcification, but it still acts with grounded force. Compassion sequesters dangerous people, it protects the vulnerable from violation, it restrains the assaults of the mean-spirited, and it speaks the truth to oppressive powers. It does so, however, with dignity. It grieves the depth of brokenness present. It refuses to hate and to demonize. It retains humanity even in the midst of the inhumane. It honors the humanity within others even when their humanity seems irredeemably hidden.

Discerning Compassionate Action

Rachel was one of the thousands celebrating Batkid during his victory parade. A software engineer, she was on her way to work when she heard reports of his heroics. She was so moved that she called her workplace, took a personal day, and joined the throngs at Union Square. As she watched Miles radiate in the chanting crowd's jubilation, she wept. She clapped, her hands held high, cheered herself hoarse, and wept. Miles's fierce battle with cancer, the city coming together in compassion, getting to be a thread within this extravagant fabric of kindness and goodwill—the entire affair pierced her heart.

Rachel was so overcome that after the rally she was unable to return to work. She walked the city in a fever of tearful euphoria and then holed up in a coffee shop in front of her laptop. She could not shake the story. She Googled every Batkid article she could find on the Internet, poring over the details and tearing up all over again. The stories and photos gave rise to a longing to do something more. She studied the Make-A-Wish Foundation website and searched for other organizations caring for terminally ill children. Those organizations so inspired her that her own work felt meaningless in comparison. She fantasized about walking away from her job and working full-time with the sick and the dying. She knew this was absurd—she would be throwing away a career she had worked toward for years—but she daydreamed all the same. She could do hospice care, hospital chaplaincy, or perhaps a Peace Corps stint overseas.

For hours, Rachel surfed the Internet, bouncing among Batkid news posts, pictures of caregivers working with children, and listings of opportunities to serve young people battling cancer. She was all but ready to submit her resignation when she realized the afternoon had turned to evening. She had lost an entire day stoking the rally's euphoria, captive to the fantasy of giving up everything to work with dying children. Brought back to reality, she was unsure what to make of what was happening within her. Clearly, quitting her job would be rash and irresponsible—she liked her work, and she had no training in caring for children. Yet, writing off the day's events and returning to work as usual felt empty and unsatisfying. Something in the faces of those children moved her. What should she do with the waves of compassion swelling up and overtaking her?

The Compassion Practice provides a path for discerning compassionate actions. Compassionate actions are those that are grounded, flow freely from the steady pulse of our core and caring Self, and nurture the pulse of restored humanity within the persons whose suffering moves us. When actions feel ungrounded, out of sync with a sustained sense of Self-presence, or out of sync with that which is truly restorative for others, they need to be reconsidered, adjusted, and perhaps deferred. Each step of the Compassion Practice helps us know when our actions flow freely with the heartbeat of care or when they are in need of realignment with the pulse of compassion. How might the Compassion Practice aid Rachel in discerning those actions that would ring true for her to embody?

First, it would invite Rachel to *catch her breath*. What began in the morning as an impulse of spontaneous compassion ended by tapping into deeper longings within her straining to get her attention. Somewhere along the way, internal movements hijacked her consciousness. Just as with more violent reactivities like rage or fantasies of revenge, the emotions of euphoria and pathos—even the fantasies of bringing love into the world—can erupt with possessive force and knock us off the ground of Self-awareness. Before leaping into any impulsive action—whether it be quitting her job, enrolling in a chaplaincy program, or slamming her laptop shut on the entire quixotic enterprise—Rachel should first seek solid ground. Catching her breath allows the flurry within her to settle. As it does, clarity emerges—not about what to do but about the internal dynamics that need to be tended before she can discern what to do.

Second, Rachel would *take her PULSE*. She would take a U-turn and notice the interior movements activated within her—the waves of tears at the sight of terminally ill children, the compelling urge to tend their wounds, the exuberant joy when they fight for life, the overwhelming impulse to quit her job and care for them full-time. She would also notice the internal voice cautioning her not to quit her job, the misgiving at being untrained for such care, and a reminder that at times she really loves the work she's already doing.

Each of these stirrings is a cry that aches to be heard. Each is rooted in some bid for life that needs to be honored and considered. Discerning compassionate action cultivates a grounded Self-awareness is free of enmeshment within any one movement and listens deeply to the underlying needs of each one. Extending Self-compassion to these underlying needs and concerns steadies the pulse of our spirits, and it helps us see what would truly satisfy the deeper yearnings within.

As Rachel listens to the underlying concerns in the flagging cries within her, what might she hear? Perhaps a *fear* that her work has lost its meaning, a *longing* to know that her generative energies touch the lives of the vulnerable in our world, an *aching wound* of a child within her who carries despair and yearns for the care that emboldens the fight for life, or the *gift* of a unique capacity she has to connect with suffering children that has never been named or cultivated. In her cautiousness, she might also hear a longing to remember the sense of meaning her current work originally gave her, a desire that her work with children engage the skills for which she is already trained, or a need that her career—whatever it may be—provides enough material stability to feed, clothe, and house herself. Listening to these stirrings with empathic understanding relaxes their intensity and grounds them in the steady pulse of Self-compassion that honors and reassures the deep need of every interior cry. Actions that are most deeply satisfying will ring true within this sense of Self-presence. If something about the action being considered feels off and eludes a sense of interior resonance, some internal concern has not been fully heard and honored.

Third, Rachel would *take the PULSE of the other*. Grounded in Self-compassion, she would turn her attention to the children whose suffering moves her and connect with the needs and yearnings within them. For what do they most deeply long? What do they most need for healing and flourishing in their lives? Which of these needs are already well tended? Which of them still cry out to be heard? Actions that are truly compassionate will be attentive to the genuine needs of those being served. Compassionate action may offer shoes to the barefoot, but it makes sure that the shoes really fit.

The needs of the suffering vary. Like the different forms that compassionate action can take, they include the needs for generosity, service, witness, solidarity, empowerment, and justice. The particular children that Rachel could meet may need, above all else, money to sustain their schooling, a few hours of caring presence, public awareness about their plight, engaging activities during long days of chemotherapy, interactive software to calibrate their medications, or advocacy for the health care denied them. Compassionate action attends to the full range of needs—soulful, social, material, and political—that nurture healing and the flourishing of life. Staying empathically attentive and connected to the needs and cries of those by whom she is moved would help Rachel discern those actions that are truly life-giving for her.

Fourth, Rachel would *decide what to do*. Of the various ways she could act on her compassion, she would discern which one to embody at the moment. That action that most rings true will resonate with both the pulse of vitality within her and the pulse of vitality aching to flourish in others. Compassionate actions restore both giver and receiver. They nurture and sustain Rachel's flourishing—they utilize her gifts, employ her skills, stimulate her creativity, invigorate her spirit, feed her soul, and deepen her sense of meaning while remaining attentive to the various needs of her general well-being. And they nurture and sustain the flourishing of others—kindling hope, easing pain, empowering resolve, extending networks of support, securing the conditions that enhance well-being, and meeting real needs. Compassionate actions lie at the intersection of life's abundance and life's diminishment. As Frederick Buechner says of vocation, they are the grounded place where our "deep gladness" meets the world's "deep hunger."[7]

As Rachel considers the compassionate actions that connect her vitality with the needs of others, various acts of care may seem appropriate. She could volunteer a few hours a week at a pediatric cancer unit while keeping her day job to support her. She could volunteer with the Make-A-Wish Foundation and turn another child's dream into reality. She could employ her software gifts for children fighting cancer in ways that have never been thought of before. Over time she may even decide to take a leave from her job and try out that stint in the Peace Corps. Whatever action she takes, however, will be deliberate, not impulsive. It will be restorative both for her and for others—gladness meeting need, life begetting life.

Discerning a particular action does not conclude the process. Rachel can return to the practice. She will recede and get grounded in the renewing springs that sustain her. She will take her PULSE, noticing and tending the stirrings within her that this act of compassion has activated. She will take the PULSE of the persons she has cared for, connecting empathically with the effects of her care and the needs and longings that still linger within them. And then she will discern the next act to take—perhaps a deepened engagement with terminally ill children, enrollment in a program for further training, or a break from it all to tend to herself with compassion.

In this way, the Compassion Practice becomes a continuing cycle. Over time, it becomes a rhythm of life. Actions give way to moments of grounding, to taking our PULSE, to taking the PULSE of others, and to discerning the subsequent restorative act. Acts of compassion give way to personifying compassion—hearts simply beating to the pulse of love.

A Coda for Batkid

After appearing on *Good Morning America* and greeting the mayor of New York, Miles Scott returned to Tulelake. He rejoined his kindergarten class and received a hero's reception. He and his parents teamed with the San Francisco 49ers Foundation to create the Batkid Fund. Through the unexpected worldwide attention, they are raising money for the same organizations that sustained Miles through his battle with cancer.[8] Miles is doing just fine, they say. And now they turn their attention to other children coping with serious illness. In this way, Batkid can now help others.

And so it goes with compassion. Compassion begs to be embodied in acts of care and kindness. Actions without compassion are empty and rote. Compassion without action is ephemeral, warm feeling dissipating into a spiritual vapor.

When embodied, however, compassion can repair the world. Just ask Batkid. He knows. Compassion received becomes compassion extended. The resuscitated pulse of life resuscitates the pulse in others. That pulse was beating in a hospital bed in rural California. It beat as well on the streets of San Francisco. Now its beat continues in hearts and hospital beds the world over.

The signs were right. Batkid rocks. He rocks to the beat of compassion.

DISCERNING A COMPASSIONATE ACTION

Deciding What to Do

1. **Catch your breath**. Ground yourself in whatever way is most helpful to you—listen to music, read a sacred text, light a candle, or sit in a settling silence. Take several deep breaths and ease into an interior space that feels safe, grounding, or sacred. Invite God's presence to hold and sustain you during this practice.

2. **Take your PULSE**. Once you have settled into a grounding interior space, consider some person or persons to whom you feel invited to extend compassion. This can be a loved one, a coworker, a stranger you've encountered during the day, or a person in your community whose suffering moves you.

   Take a moment and turn inward. Notice what interior movements stir within as you consider the person in your awareness. Welcome and hold any that are there. You might experience pity, fear, anxiety, discomfort at his or her distress, or perhaps measures of your own grief and pain. Assure these interior movements that you are aware that they are present for a reason, and if they prove to be tenacious, you will ponder them more fully. Then invite them to relax so you can be genuinely open and attentive to the person in your awareness.

3. Take the other's PULSE.

Paying attention. In your imagination, turn your attention toward the person you feel invited to extend compassion. For a few moments, simply pay attention without judgment to what he or she is doing and the particular way that he or she is doing it as if your observation went without notice.

Understanding empathically. While you continue to gaze upon him or her, cultivate a deeper understanding of the soulful cry hidden within his or her emotions or behaviors. Use the FLAG questions to cultivate this understanding.

> What *fears* does he or she carry?

> What *longings* pulsate within him or her?

> What *aching wounds* haunt him or her?

> What is his or her hidden and thwarted *gift* yearning to flourish?

Loving with connection. Let yourself feel a sense of compassionate connection to this person. Simply love or care for him or her just as you would love a wounded or frightened child who needs care.

Sensing the sacredness. If it feels right, notice if God's presence feels near and invite that presence—as Jesus, Mary, a symbol of the Holy Spirit, the warmth of God's light—to be with this person at the source of his or her suffering, tending to him or her in whatever way feels healing and restoring.

Embodying new life. Let yourself embrace the new life that yearns to be birthed within the person.

4. **Decide what to do.** Brainstorm various compassionate actions you might embody toward this person. Consider each of the following types of actions and try to list one, two, or even several possible actions under each category.

> Acts of generosity

> Acts of service

> Acts of witness

> Acts of solidarity

> Acts of empowerment

> Acts of justice

Of the various actions that have come to you, be aware of those that most attract, energize, intrigue, or surprise you. Consider that action in light of the signposts of the Compassion Practice:

> Does this action seem to flow from and sustain your own sense of personal and sacred groundedness?

> Does this action promote and preserve the flourishing of your own humanity? Does it flow from your own sense of personal power? Does it maintain and enhance your own human dignity? Does it employ your own unique gifts, skills, and resources? Can you engage in this action without other interior movements becoming activated?

> Does this action promote and preserve the flourishing of the other? Does it maintain and enhance his or her dignity? Does it meet him or her at the source of his or her deepest and most life-giving needs? Does it contribute to his or her sense of personal power? Does it invite any appropriate need for accountability and restoration?

After pondering these considerations, discern which action feels most resonant with these signposts. What action do you feel most invited to embody toward this person? Which action feels most right?

As a final consideration, imagine yourself engaging in this act of compassion. Like watching a movie, see yourself speaking the words or undertaking the compassionate action that you feel called to embody. Notice what reactions are stirred within you, and sense if they resonate compassion. Notice the effect the action has on the other person, and sense if it resonates compassion. If it continues to feel right, extend this compassion into the future encounter you intend to have with this person. Then embody the action itself.

DISCERNING A COMPASSIONATE ACTION

Secret Acts of Compassion for Others

This exercise invites you first to increase your awareness of the various persons in your day—the grocery clerk, the elderly woman who lives down the street, the garbage collector, the bus driver, the man drinking coffee by himself at a coffee shop, a coworker, a family member. Keep your heart and eyes open as you go through the day, and notice the persons you typically encounter. Then choose one person to give your attention to. To whom are you most drawn? Who attracts your curiosity?

As you focus your attention on this person, connect briefly with the PULSE of humanity that beats within him or her in that moment.

> Pay attention to what he or she is doing and how.

> Understand his or her fears, longings, aches, and stifled gifts.

> Love him or her with a quiet sense of connection.

> Sense the sacredness that holds him or her with compassion.

> Embody the new life that yearns to flourish within him or her.

Behold the person and his or her PULSE while allowing compassion to rise within you. Then listen for an act of kindness that you might undertake toward this person. Maybe you leave a note of gratitude for a server. Or maybe you anonymously pick up the check for a person getting coffee. Maybe you get up early and shovel the snow from your neighbor's sidewalk. Or maybe you leave freshly baked cookies for the postal worker. Allow your imagination to uncover some secret, anonymous act of compassion to engage in.

After you have completed your secret compassionate act, reflect on your experience. How did you feel afterward? What are you like when you engage in an act of compassion and kindness?

The Hope

The Miracle of Compassion

Mike was a man who hated Christmas. He believed it brought out the worst in people—the whole greedy lot of them. "When I was young," he grumbled, "Christmas was all about giving. Now it's all about getting. Getting all the toys that you want. Getting to all the sales before others. Getting a bigger bonus than the one you got last year. And I am sick of it. From now on, I want nothing for Christmas. No chocolate samplers, no polyester ties, no bottles of cheap cologne. Until people recognize what Christmas is all about, I don't want to get a thing."

Nan, Mike's wife of some forty-eight years, was worried about him. She worried that his retirement years would be devoured by daytime TV and recliner passivity. And she worried that his cantankerousness would harden and choke off the caring man she knew Mike to be. Surely Christmas, of all times of the year, should be a season in which care could win out over crankiness. And then she got an idea.

The idea came to Nan when she and Mike were watching their grandson's wrestling match. A team of underprivileged teens was in the tournament too. The members of the team were easy to pick out—their uniforms were ragged, their T-shirts threadbare, their sweatpants ill fitting, either too big or too small. And they were being crushed by all of the wealthier schools with crisp, color-coordinated wrestling gear.

"Just look at those boys," Mike bemoaned. "It just isn't right. This sport may be all those boys really have. Sure they jump up after losing, but being beaten down over and over again—why it'll take the heart right out of you."

That Christmas, Nan did something different. She tucked a single envelope with Mike's name on it between a few ornaments on the tree. On Christmas morning, after all of the other presents were opened, Nan feigned surprise and said, "Why there's still one more present. And, sweetheart, it has your name on it."

Mike griped, "I thought I said I didn't want anything this year."

"Maybe you'll like this," she prodded.

He took the envelope, eyed it suspiciously, and opened it. Inside was a simple index card. Typed on it was a pledge. During the coming year, Nan would devote her considerable seamstress skills to making wrestling uniforms for the inner-city school the two of them had watched earlier. Mike read it and mumbled, "Well, at least it's not a box of peanut brittle."

Early in January, Nan stayed true to her word. She set up a sewing station in the family room and began sketching uniform designs. After a while, Mike wandered over and glanced at the sketches. He shook his head and scowled, "No, no, no, wrestling uniforms don't look anything like that. Besides, the colors are all wrong. And the sizes, how will you know the sizes unless you know the players?"

"Well, I was wondering about that," Nan admitted. "Do you think you could help me?"

Quicker than a takedown, Mike was off. He went to the school to measure the youngsters. He went to the fabric store to pick out material. He joined Nan in the family room, separating fronts from backs and pinning numbers into place.

Of course, more trips to the school were needed. The kids, beside themselves at the idea of new uniforms, begged to be part of the project. Soon, they were selling chocolate bars to buy headgear and scheduling twice-a-day workouts to break in the new equipment. The team adopted Mike and Nan as unofficial team mascots. Mike and Nan took their commitment to the boys seriously and chaperoned away games. They organized a field trip to a tournament at the local university. Mike even took a turn as assistant coach for a day. Sure, he couldn't wrestle like he used to, but he still knew a thing or two about half nelsons and three-point stances.

Mike had so much fun that once the year passed and many of the boys graduated, he started poking around the Christmas tree. His grimace had a glint. "I wonder," he toyed, "if there might be something for me this year." And there was.

Mike and Nan began a new family tradition. Every Christmas played out to the same script. After all the other presents were opened and discarded, Nan would discover a single white envelope lodged in the branches of the tree. With mock surprise she would announce, "Why, Mike, there seems to be something for you after all this year."

Mike would jump up, eye the envelope suspiciously, and muse, "I hope it's not a box of peanut brittle." And it never was. The envelope would hold an index card pledging some project for Mike and Nan to do together during the coming year.

One year Mike and Nan worked at a boys' home designing a playground, organizing car washes to fund it, and mobilizing volunteers to begin its construction. Another year, they galvanized a group of neighborhood children to build birdhouses and feeding stations for wildlife at a local marshland. And one year, they took on city hall. With a band of budding activists, they protested a zoning decision and transformed a vacant lot into a community garden.

Year after year, Mike and Nan carried on. Simple acts of kindness took root throughout the city—at community centers and juvenile halls, at charter schools and children's homes. Each act was germinated by the seed of a single envelope resting on the branch of a Christmas tree. Those envelopes brought life—not only to the town but also to Mike. As Nan would later reflect, "Those were the best years of our lives."

One year, just a few days before Christmas, Mike suffered a stroke and died in his sleep. From all over, family, both close and extended, gathered to attend the Christmas Eve funeral and stay with Nan through her holiday grief. With all of the company, Nan managed to keep herself occupied throughout the day on Christmas Eve. After the funeral, there were meals to cook and linens to put out. As evening approached, there were dishes to wash and coffee to serve. As was her way, Nan rebuffed pleas for her to sit down. And even as the others went to bed, Nan busied herself straightening chairs and setting out breakfast dishes until she and her daughter were the only two still up.

"Mom, it's late, and the kids will be up early. Why don't you get some sleep."

"You go ahead," Nan insisted. "There's a couple more things I want to get done."

"Okay, Mom, but promise me you'll be in bed soon."

"Of course." With a knowing hug, the daughter went to bed.

Nan dug out a few more presents from the closets and stuffed the children's stockings. She checked the Christmas ham and set the timer for the coffee pot. She wiped down the kitchen counters and locked the back door. Then she switched off the lights room by room until the only light came from the glow of the Christmas tree. And for the first time that day, Nan stopped.

Memories adorned the tree as much as the ornaments. There was the metallic blue ball—the only ornament that hung on the barren tree of Nan and Mike's very first Christmas. There was the embroidered pink cradle with *Baby's First Christmas* lettered on the side. There was the pale green Statue of Liberty, its torch lit red, that Mike just had to have on their trip to New York City. For some time, Nan simply sat and stared, fragments of memories passing before her.

And then, as was Nan's custom, she pulled open the drawer of the end table beside her, and slipped out of a sewing magazine something that had been placed there several weeks earlier. A single white envelope addressed with two words: For Mike. She stared at the envelope for a long time. Then she slid it deep into the branches of the tree.

"This is for you, sweetheart," she whispered. "This is for you."

She pulled the plug on the tree lights and climbed the stairs to bed.

The next morning, squeals from downstairs woke Nan. She had slept longer than she wanted. The rest of the family was already huddled around the tree. She could hear one of her grandkids plead, "When will she be up?"

"Don't worry," a mother reassured. "Grandma will be down soon."

With that cue, Nan donned her robe and slippers and went downstairs. A chorus of greetings rose from the faces that filled her living room.

"Merry Christmas, Mom."

"Merry Christmas, Grandma."

The kids were giddy, and signs of Santa's presence were scattered throughout the room. The tree was lit in all of its festive glory.

And then Nan stopped.

Something was off. It was the tree. It was wrapped in white. Not white lights but white paper. The tree was laden with dozens of white envelopes. All the family members—each daughter and son, granddaughter and grandson, niece, nephew, and cousin—had placed their own envelope on the tree, their own pledge to a project of kindness in memory of Grandpa Mike.

Perched on her stairs that Christmas morning, Nan could already see the ripples of care reaching out into the world. She still ached for Mike. But her grief was eased as she saw not only those Christmas envelopes but also the envelopes multiplying through time on Christmas trees in the future.

And Nan knew how pleased Mike would be. He was, after all, a man who loved Christmas.

The Miracle of Compassion

Sometimes the way of radical compassion gives rise to extraordinary acts of courageous care: warriors of compassion reaching out to racist segregationists, violent extremists, and the teens who killed their own children. Sometimes radical compassion calls for something as simple as an index card of kindness lodged in the branches of a Christmas tree. Either way, acts of compassion shimmer with the miraculous.

In a world where abuse bleeds into our homes, our schools, and our sacred institutions; where violence and poverty ravage our cities and neighborhoods; where venom and vitriol permeate our public discourse—any act of kindness and care offers a wondrous assertion of humanity within the insidious encroachment of the inhumane.

It is a miracle that a man would forgive his son's killer and invite him to join forces in a campaign to eradicate youth violence. It is a miracle that a city would conspire to celebrate the superhero inside of a child standing up to cancer. It is a miracle that an aging wife would see the caring man within her embittered husband and partner with him to complete projects of compassion throughout their final years together.

These are not the spectacular miracles of parting the Red Sea or of Jesus rising from the dead. They are ordinary miracles—coming from the hands of grandparents, wrestling coaches, mothers, and software engineers. Yet, they are miracles all the same.

These acts interrupt the cycles of fear, retreat, attack, and retaliation that play out in our lives with instinctive tenacity. They soften the hearts of those who are hardened, restoring them to their humanity. And they pulsate with the living presence of the One who gave his life for love.

Compassion bears resurrection power.

Jesus' way of radical compassion aligns our spirit with the Divine Spirit that brings life out of death, hope in the face of despair, love within the lethal contagion of hate in our world. As sure as the night gives way to the dawn, all creation is held within the heartbeat of God that pulsates new life into our planet. And God's heart beats to the pulse of compassion. When we embody love and mercy, we live in union with God. Our hearts beat as one with the sacred heartbeat that sustains and resuscitates all life.

Each act of care we incarnate—be it simple or radical—is the gift we bear from the God whose heart holds everything and everyone. It is the index card of sacred kindness that we slip into the branches of our broken and beaten-up planet. And when we do so, we can trust that it does not sit there idly. God's Spirit is at work within it. It multiplies. In the morning, we will see. Envelopes of compassion will encompass our world.

Leader's Guide

Welcome to the leader's guide for *Compassion in Practice: The Way of Jesus.* This guide includes six sessions. Each session includes stories illustrating the teaching points, questions for discussion, contemplative practices, and an invitation for reflection for the following session.

You need not feel obligated to follow every aspect of this guide; use it as a tool in any way that works best to support you as you lead your group through the book. For example, we encourage you to either share your own personal stories as examples of the teaching points or select stories from the book. Of those discussion questions offered, choose only those relevant and appropriate to your group.

This guide works best if group participants read the book chapters to be discussed prior to each session. You might want to check that all participants have a copy of the book and suggest that books be brought along to the session gatherings. You may reassure participants that if they miss a session, they will not be behind for the following session. Each section can be covered as a stand-alone piece.

An overall checklist with materials you will need for the sessions is included in this guide. Materials necessary for specific sessions are located in the guide for that particular section.

Through this guide, we hope to share the message of Jesus' way of radical love and compassion. Thank you for making the space and time to guide your group through *Compassion in Practice: The Way of Jesus.*

Leader's Checklist for Each Session

> Review the entire chapter until you understand the flow of the chapter, teaching points, and practices. Be ready to share instructions for the group in your own words.

> Decide if you want to use a story of your own to illustrate the teaching points. If so, practice on your own ahead of time.

> Decide whether you will lead the practices. If so, practice on your own prior to the group session.

> Decide which discussion questions you will use.

Materials Needed

> Name badges

> Felt pens for writing names

> Copies for each participant of any of the practices you will lead

> iPod or equivalent to play music, if desired

> Small table or altar with appropriate materials (for example, a candle, candleholder or plate, matches, sacred objects to place on the altar)

> Flip chart or whiteboard with pens

> A bell for gathering participants together

Setup

Place chairs in a semicircle or horseshoe arrangement with the flip chart or whiteboard at the head of the space. Create a sacred space at the center with a small table, a candle, matches, a cross, and/or other sacred objects.

Small-Group Guidelines

During the sessions, you may want to break into small groups if your overall group is larger than six or eight. We find groups between four and six people to be most effective. The purpose of these groups is to find companions along the way, something like compassion support groups. For these groups to function in this way, it is important that each participant feels safe within the group. To facilitate, we suggest the following guidelines:

> Don't cross-talk.

> Ask for confidentiality.

> Listen without judgment or critique.

> Don't give advice.

After going through these guidelines, ask the large group for any other suggestions that would help people feel safe within their small group. Affirm the suggestions that come from the group. When all have been shared, ask the participants if everyone could agree to these guidelines for the duration of the program.

Sample Lesson Time Line

> Opening prayer or moment of silence

> Summarize the teaching points and discuss teaching stories: 25 minutes

> Contemplative practice and/or personal story sharing: 25 minutes

> Final group debriefing (including assignment and invitation for the week that follows): 10 minutes

> Closing prayer

Session 1: *Jesus' Spiritual Path of Compassion*

In the introduction, we read stories of Jesus' ongoing and radical compassion for all; we read of a loving God who delights in our joy and weeps with us in our sorrow. We introduced the idea that compassion starts with self-compassion and that when we have tools and practices to cultivate self-compassion, we are in a space that frees us to extend compassion to others, even those whom we find difficult. We briefly introduced the threefold path of compassion: "Jesus' spiritual path of radical compassion has three dimensions: a deepening of our connection to the compassion of God, a restoration to a humanity fully loved and alive, and an increase to our capacity to be instruments of compassion toward others in the world. These three movements flow from the heartbeat of God" (21–22). The stories from this chapter illustrated examples of radically inclusive compassion.

Session Outline

Reminder: Choose and adapt what is most appropriate and helpful of the following suggestions.

> Begin the session with a moment of prayer or silence to ground the group.

> Review, summarize, and discuss the main points of the chapter with the group. Use the following discussion questions:
>> Did anything in the chapter surprise you?
>> What in the chapter resonated with your experience?
>> What in the chapter challenged you?
>> In what ways do you see Jesus as an example of compassion?
>> How can Jesus' spiritual path be summed up as a way of compassion?

> Discuss the stories from the book, or share a story of your own to illustrate the points of the chapter.
>> The Yellow Ribbons (14–15)

    How was this an example of radical compassion?

    What must that moment have been like for the man on the bus when he saw the oak tree festooned with yellow ribbons?

    How is this a parable of God's love?

>> A Garden of Compassion (23–24)

    How did Raul Torres bring compassion to life?

    How was he an example of radical compassion?

    What affect did his compassion have on the boy's life?

> Ask the group to break into pairs or small groups, or do this practice as a whole group. If working in small groups, give the groups enough time for each person to share his or her example. Then bring the whole group back together to discuss the examples.

> Invite participants to share one person from history or their own life experience who offers an inspiring example of the kind of radical compassion Jesus teaches.

> Ask the participants to read chapter 1 for the next session.

> End the session with the following invitation: Notice simple moments of kindness and compassion throughout the week.

> Lead a closing prayer, or ask a member of the group to lead a prayer.

Session 2: *The Pulse of Compassion*

In chapter 1, we learned that compassion is "simply being moved in our depths by others' experience and responding in a way that intends either to ease their suffering or promote their flourishing" (30) and that "contemplative awareness, as Walter J. Burghardt classically defined it, entails 'a long, loving look at the real'" (31). We learned about the following six dimensions that constitute compassion (34):

Paying attention (or contemplative awareness)

Understanding empathically (or empathic care)

Loving with connection (or all-accepting presence)

Sensing the sacredness (or spiritual expansiveness)

Embodying new life (or desire for flourishing)

Discerning compassionate action

We also learned of the fourfold rhythm of compassion: "deepening our connection with the expansive compassion of God, cultivating a self-compassion that recalibrates our erratic pulse to the steady pulse of our restored humanity, cultivating a compassion for the suffering that afflicts someone's humanity, and responding with concrete acts of embodied care and connection" (35). These are the four steps of the Compassion Practice:

1. Catch your breath (Get grounded)

2. Take your PULSE (Cultivate compassion for yourself)

3. Take the other's PULSE (Cultivate compassion for another)

4. Decide what to do (Discern compassionate action)

Session Outline

Reminder: Choose and adapt what is most appropriate and helpful of the following suggestions.

› Begin the session with a moment of prayer or silence to ground the group.

› Review, summarize, and discuss the main points of the chapter with the group. Use the following discussion questions:

  › Did anything in the chapter surprise you?

  › What in the chapter resonated with your experience?

  › What in the chapter challenged you?

  › What did you learn about the nature of compassion?

  › How is compassion rooted in the heart?

› Discuss the stories from the book, or share a story of your own to illustrate the six dimensions of compassion and/or the four steps of the Compassion Practice.

  › Azim Khamisa and Tony Hicks (28–29)

    How did Khamisa embody the six elements of compassion?

    How did Khamisa embody each of the four steps of the Compassion Practice?

> Invite each participant to share one story of their own when someone expressed compassion to them. Participants can share these stories either in the large group or in their small groups from the previous week. After sharing, ask them to discuss how these acts of compassion embodied the six dimensions of the PULSE of compassion.

> Ask participants to read chapter 2 for the next session.

> End the session with the following invitation: Ask the group to practice Connecting with Your Breath (61–62) at home. Invite participants to notice when they get activated. In response, they can simply catch their breath as the first step of the Compassion Practice.

> Lead a closing prayer, or ask a member of the group to lead a prayer.

Session 3: *Catching Our Breath*

In chapter 2, we learned tangible ways to catch our breath in the midst of triggers, reactivities, and difficult others (48). We learned of Martin Luther King Jr.'s compassion toward a man who attacked him in Birmingham, Alabama (42–44). We learned more about awareness as the first step of the Compassion Practice and how this helps us to ground ourselves in times of difficulty (45–49). We were reminded too of the importance of remembering ourselves as beloved (49–51) and knowing ourselves beloved by God (51–53). We saw how others who show us love and compassion kindle our belovedness and how the act of self-care gives us a way to support our sense of belovedness for ourselves.

Session Outline

Reminder: Choose and adapt what is most appropriate and helpful of the following suggestions.

> Begin the session with a moment of prayer or silence to ground the group.

> Review, summarize, and discuss the main points of the chapter with the group. Use the following discussion questions:

> Did anything in the chapter surprise you?

> What in the chapter resonated with your experience?

> What in the chapter challenged you?

> Why is grounding important for ourselves and our relationships?

> How do people ground themselves when they are activated?

> Invite any questions or surprises from the reading or practices at home.

> Discuss one of the stories below, or share one of your own to illustrate a sacred moment that grounds you in the truth of what you know about God's love and compassion.

> Martin Luther King Jr. in Birmingham, Alabama (42–44)

What made MLK's response of love and compassion toward hatred possible?

How does this story exemplify radical compassion?

> Raul Monroe's Dad (49–50)

How is this story a parable about God's care for and delight in God's beloved creation?

Does this story remind you of times when someone has reveled in your belovedness, seen, and celebrated you, as Raul's dad did? How were those moments parables of how God sees you?

> Joey and Danny (53–55)

What does this story reveal about your longing for and your need for compassion?

What would you say to Joey? What would God say to Joey?

> Harry's Fortieth Anniversary (56–59)

How did Harry's experience of radical hospitality affect his image of heaven?

How does Harry's anniversary experience inform his daily practice of Eucharist and his trips to the retirement community?

❭ Invite the group to reflect on the extravagant love of God, who says to Jesus, "I am your father" in the face of Jesus being negatively referred to as "the son of Mary" (52).

❭ As a group, brainstorm ways to stay grounded in awareness, catch your breath, and connect with your belovedness in difficult moments. Write suggestions on a flip-chart or whiteboard.

❭ Lead the group in the Remembering Sacred Moments practice (63–64).

❭ Following the practice, divide into small groups or stay in the larger group. Invite each person to share the story he or she reflected on. Then debrief the practice together.

   ❭ Ask the following questions: What do these moments say about who God is and what God is like? What practices and activities help you remember and stay connected to the God you experienced in these moments?

❭ Ask the participants to read chapter 3 for the next session.

❭ End the session with the following invitation: Try the Remembering Sacred Moments practice at home.

❭ Lead a closing prayer, or ask a member of the group to lead a prayer.

Session 4: *Taking Our PULSE*

In chapter 3, we learned how to cultivate and recover compassion for ourselves. We learned that Jesus teaches a path of personal restoration (66–67). We read about the concept of self and how our true nature is one that is compassionate at its core (67–68). We also learned about two ways of being in the world: grounded and centered or knocked off-center by interior movements (68–71). We learned of Jesus' radical practice of compassion, how to take the U-turn (71–73), and that interior movements are cries for compassion (73–75). Also, the FLAG practice was introduced (77).

Session Outline

Reminder: Choose and adapt what is most appropriate and helpful of the following suggestions.

> Begin the session with a moment of prayer or silence to ground the group.

> Review, summarize, and discuss the main points of the chapter with the group. Use the following discussion questions:

> > Did anything in the chapter surprise you?

> > What in the chapter resonated with your experience?

> > What in the chapter challenged you?

> > How are your interior movements the suffering cries within you aching to be heard?

> > How does taking your PULSE tend to these cries and restore you to your true Self?

> Discuss the stories from the book, or share a story of your own when you embodied your true self or a story of taking a U-turn and recalibrating your pulse after being triggered.

> > The Woman in the St. Louis Mall (65–66)

> > Describe the woman's appearance when she embodied her true Self.

> > How does she reflect the two ways of being in the world?

> > Justin Borrows the Car (70–73)

> > How does this story embody the first two steps of the Compassion Practice—getting grounded and taking your own pulse through self-compassion?

What are some ways you can calm yourself and catch your
breath when you are triggered by interior movements?

> Lead the group in the Welcoming Presence Meditation (80–82) or in
Deepening Your Understanding of an Interior Movement (83–84).

> Following the practice, divide into small groups or stay in the larger
group. Invite each person to share either his or her experience of the practice or one interior movement in his or her life that is the cry of a deeper
need. Then debrief the exercise together.

> Ask the participants to read chapter 4 for the next session.

> End the session with the following invitation: Try either of the exercises
from chapter 3 in order to notice and be aware of interior movements that
become activated within you and threaten to hijack you.

> Lead a closing prayer, or ask a member of the group to lead a prayer.

Session 5: *Taking Their PULSE*

In chapter 4, we learned that Jesus' path of radical compassion extends to
others as well as to ourselves. We can use the PULSE practice to connect
with, be open to, and act compassionately toward others. When we do not
feel open to extending compassion to others, we are invited to tend to our
own interior movements and wounds through the various practices, especially PULSE and the U-turn. We are reminded of the belovedness of
others. Knowledge of this belovedness deepens our connection to others and
to God (88–89). Everyone—even those we find the most difficult—contains
the pulse of humanity and the capacity for care, connection, and compassion. The undesirable actions of others are FLAGs longing for compassion. The path of compassion neither condones violation nor minimizes the
suffering of those who feel violated. It does, however, offer the invitation for
us to see the wound underneath the violating actions. We learned how to
cultivate compassion toward others, even our enemies. We also learned that
our enemies are our spiritual teachers and mirrors of parts of ourselves that

cause us pain or shame. Like us, our enemies are filled with unmet needs and unfulfilled gifts.

Session Outline

Reminder: Choose and adapt what is most appropriate and helpful of the following suggestions.

> Begin the session with a moment of prayer or silence to ground the group.

> Review, summarize, and discuss the main points of the chapter with the group. Use the following discussion questions:

   > Did anything in the chapter surprise you?

   > What in the chapter resonated with your experience?

   > What in the chapter challenged you?

   > In cultivating compassion for others, why must you first take your own PULSE to be open to a compassionate connection with someone else?

   > How does taking someone else's PULSE open up compassion within you for him or her?

> Discuss one of the stories below, or share a story of your own to illustrate someone embodying compassion toward another.

   > Wheelchair Dancing (85)

      How does the therapist embody the PULSE of compassion?

      Describe a time when you saw someone embodying kindness and simple compassion.

   > Damian (89–90)

      How would you describe Damian's true Self?

      What does this story suggest about how our compassionate Self becomes hardened and buried? How can it be reawakened?

      How can we reignite the spark of another's sense of worth?

> Misty's Ashes (92–95)

How is aggressive behavior a FLAG of a deeper cry?

Reflect on ways of calming and grounding yourself in difficult encounters with others so that you can be open to their stories as well as your own.

> An Enemy Transformed on the Softball Field (102–4)

How did the author's "enemy" mirror his own pain, shame, and unmet needs?

How do your enemies mirror your pain, shame, unmet needs, or unfulfilled gifts?

> Lead the group in Hearing the Cry of a Beloved or Friendly Other (105–6) or The Compassion Practice with a Difficult Other (107–10).

> Following the practice, divide into small groups or stay in the larger group. Invite each person to share either his or her experience of the practice or the pulse of humanity that beats within the person they have been beholding. Then debrief the practice together.

> Ask the participants to read chapter 5 and The Hope for the next session.

> End the session with the following invitation: Think of one person through the week toward whom you would like to extend compassion.

> Lead a closing prayer, or ask a member of the group to lead a prayer.

Session 6: *Deciding What to Do* and *The Miracle of Compassion*

In chapter 5 and the conclusion, we learned about the restorative power of compassionate action. This action is more than sentimental; it is concrete, embodied, and active. Compassionate action is contagious and it restores us. We learned that Jesus' radical compassion is love, which is embodied "through concrete actions that aim to ease the pain of those who suffer and

promote the flourishing of life for all" (116). We serve Jesus when we engage
in acts of compassion in its many forms. We can engage in empowered acts
of compassion in the midst of violence through social action and nonviolent empowered compassion. We learned that an eye for an eye, loving your
enemies, turning the other cheek, and going another mile are acts of standing up to injustice (118–24). We found that compassionate action is transformative, and we learned how to discern and put empowered compassion
into action. We learned that radical, engaged compassion is grounded in
God's love as the source of our truth. Empowered compassion promotes and
preserves the flourishing of the victim's humanity, recognizes the humanity
and dignity of the other, and invites the offender into right and appropriate
relationship (124–30). We celebrated the miracle of compassion.

Materials Needed

> Index cards

> Pens

> Envelopes

Session Outline

Reminder: Choose and adapt what is most appropriate and helpful of the
following suggestions.

> Begin the session with a moment of prayer or silence to ground the group.

> Review, summarize, and discuss the main points of the chapter with the
  group. Use the following discussion questions:

  > Did anything in the chapter surprise you?

  > What in the chapter resonated with your experience?

  > What in the chapter challenged you?

  > What are different ways that compassion can be embodied?

  > What is the relationship between compassion and accountability when
    people are engaged in violent or abusive behavior?

> Discuss the section that explains Jesus' radical, nonviolent, and compassionate intentions of turning the other cheek (120–22), going an extra mile (122–23), and giving your cloak as well (123).

> > How is this interpretation of Jesus' teaching different than other interpretations of it?

> > In what ways does it surprise you?

> > How is this interpretation an example of empowerment and not submissiveness?

> Discuss the stories from the book, or share a story of your own to illustrate the points of the chapter.

> > The Adventures of Batkid (111–14)

> > > What did the story reveal about ways to embody compassion?

> > > How did compassionate action restore those involved?

> > > What compassionate action can you take in your community?

> > The Folktale of the Enemy Merchants (120–21)

> > > What did the story reveal about the cycle of violence?

> > > What are contemporary examples of cycles of violence?

> > Mawanda from Zimbabwe (125–26)

> > > How does Mawanda embody both compassion and empowerment?

> > > How does she remember the truth of who she is in God's eyes even when powerful forces try to diminish her?

> > > How can you stand up to injustice within your community?

> > Mike and Nan's Christmas Notes (141–45)

> > > How can compassion be contagious?

In what ways can you bring the Compassion Practice to life in your home, community, and church?

> Lead the group in Deciding What to Do (136–38) or Secret Acts of Compassion for Others (139–40).

> Invite each member to share, either in the large group or a small group, one act of kindness and compassion he or she feels moved to embody within his or her life.

GOING FORTH

The last act on this journey of radical compassion together is to bless and commission compassionate actions that will be embodied in our lives.

> Option 1: As a group, choose a wound in the world and reflect on what compassionate action can be taken together to ease this wound.

> Option 2: After each person has identified an act of compassion he or she feels moved to embody in his or her life, ask each person to write his or her pledge on an index card and place it on the altar during a final time of prayer.

> Option 3: Pass out index cards and envelopes to the group. Invite the participants to self-address the envelope, print on the index card an act of compassion they feel moved to embody, and write a compassionate letter to themselves. Collect the envelopes and mail them to participants four weeks after the last session.

> Discern whether the group would like to continue meeting. How could the group engage in acts of compassion together or individually?

Notes

The Invitation

1. Evelyn Underhill, *The Spiritual Life* (London: Hodder & Stoughton, 1937), 15, 74–75; Thomas Merton, *New Seeds of Contemplation* (New York: New Directions Publishing Corporation, 1961), 297; Matthew Fox, OP, *Illuminations of Hildegard of Bingen* (Santa Fe, NM: Bear & Company, 1985).

2. Karen Armstrong, *Twelve Steps to a Compassionate Life* (New York: Alfred A. Knopf, 2010), 4.

3. One source for this legend is Armstrong, *Twelve Steps*, 50–51.

4. J. Francis Stroud, SJ, *Praying Naked: The Spirituality of Anthony de Mello, SJ* (New York: Image Books, 2005), 41.

5. Sandra Lommasson, "Widening the Tent: Spiritual Practice Across Traditions," in *Sacred Is the Call: Formation and Transformation in Spiritual Direction Programs*, Suzanne Buckley, ed. (New York: Crossroad Publishing Company, 2005), 164.

6. Due to the sexist and hierarchical connotations of the word *kingdom*, Ada Maria Isasi-Diaz coined the term, *kin-dom*. See Isasi-Diaz, "Solidarity: Love of Neighbor in the 1980s" in *Lift Every Voice: Constructing Christian Theologies from the Underside*, Susan Brooks Thistlthwaite and Mary Potter Engel, eds., (San Francisco: HarperSanFrancisco, 1990), 31–40, 303–5.

7. Marcus J. Borg, *Jesus, A New Vision: Spirit, Culture, and the Life of Discipleship* (San Francisco: HarperSanFrancisco, 1987), 125–49.

8. It is worth noting that worship bears this same threefold rhythm. We gather within sacred space; we are replenished in word and sacrament; and we are sent forth to love and serve the world—only to return once more to be replenished and sent forth.

Chapter 1: The Pulse of Compassion

1. Azim Khamisa, *From Murder to Forgiveness: A Father's Journey* (Bloomington, IN: Balboa Press, 2012). For information on the Tariq Khamisa Foundation, see www.tkf.org.

2. Some suggest that the heart's movement in compassion is more than metaphorical. See, for example, Doc Lew Childre, Howard Martin, and Donna Beech, *The HeartMath Solution: The Institute of HeartMath's Revolutionary Program for Engaging the Power of the Heart's Intelligence* (San Francisco: HarperOne, 2000). Ilia Delio, OSF cites Mary Jo Meadows definition of compassion as "the quivering of the heart in response to another's suffering," *Compassion: Living in the Spirit of St. Francis* (Cincinnati, OH: St. Anthony Messenger Press, 2011), 47.

3. Burghardt adapted this phrase from one by contemplative Carmelite Father William McNamara. See Walter J. Burghardt, "Contemplation: A Long, Loving Look at the Real," *Church* (Winter 1989): 14–18.

4. See, for example, Phyllis Trible, *God and the Rhetoric of Sexuality* (Philadelphia: Fortress Press, 1978), 31–59; and *Theological Dictionary of the New Testament*, vol. VII, Geoffrey W. Bromiley, trans. and ed. (Grand Rapids, MI: Eerdmans Publishing Company, 1971), 553–57.

5. See David J. Wallin, *Attachment in Psychotherapy* (New York: The Guilford Press, 2007), 106, and Daniel J. Siegel, *The Developing Mind: How Relationships and the Brain Interact to Shape Who We Are* (New York: The Guilford Press, 2001).

6. Though the phrase "U-turn" has been used in numerous contexts, I first read it in Richard C. Schwartz, *You Are the One You've Been Waiting For: Bringing Courageous Love to Intimate Relationships* (Oak Park, IL: Trailheads Publications, 2008).

Chapter 2: Catching Our Breath

1. The primary source for this story and King's words, which he paraphrased, is William Johnston, *King* (New York: Warner Books, Inc., 1978), 141–43. See also, Taylor Branch, *Parting the Waters: America in the King Years 1954–1963* (New York: Simon and Schuster, 1989).

2. For an excellent source on the physiological dimensions of breathing and well-being, see Alane Daugherty, *The Power Within: From Neuroscience to Transformation* (Dubuque, IA: Kendall Hunt Publishing, 2008), 114–43, and Alane Daugherty, *From Mindfulness to Heartfulness: A Journey of Transformation through the Science of Embodiment* (Bloomington, IN: Balboa Press, 2014), 164–65.

3. Anthony de Mello, *Sadhana, a Way to God: Christian Exercises in Eastern Form* (Garden City, NY: Image Books, 1984), 28. See also, Thich Nhat Hanh *Breathe, You Are Alive!: Sutra on the Full Awareness of Breathing* (Berkeley, CA: Parallax Press, 1996).

4. John Makransky, *Awakening Through Love: Unveiling Your Deepest Goodness* (Boston: Wisdom Publications, 2007), 22.

5. Dennis Linn, Sheila Fabricant Linn, and Matthew Linn, *Sleeping with Bread: Holding What Gives You Life* (Mahwah, NJ: Paulist Press, 1995).

6. See, for example, "Breathing the Name of God," in Lawrence Kushner, *Eyes Remade for Wonder: A Lawrence Kushner Reader* (Woodstock, VT: Jewish Lights Publishing, 1998), 144.

7. Gabriel Galache, SJ, *Praying Body and Soul: Methods and Practices of Anthony de Mello* (New York: Crossroad Publishing Company, 1998), 19.

8. See Kabir's poem "Professional Counseling" in Daniel Ladinsky, trans., *Love Poems from God: Twelve Sacred Voices from the East and West* (New York: Penguin Compass, 2002).

9. See Stephen Mitchell, *The Gospel According to Jesus: A New Translation and Guide to His Essential Teachings for Believers and Unbelievers* (New York: HarperPerennial, 1993), 19–36.

10. Helpful descriptions of breath prayers can be found in de Mello, *Sadhana*; Hanh, *Breathe, You Are Alive!*; and Tilden Edwards, *Living in the Presence: Spiritual Exercises to Open Your Life to the Awareness of God* (New York: HarperCollins, 1995).

Chapter 3: Taking Our PULSE

1. Richard C. Schwartz, *Introduction to the Internal Family Systems Model* (Oak Park, IL: Trailheads Publications, 2001); Richard C. Schwartz, *Internal Family Systems Therapy* (New York: The Guilford Press, 1995). For Merton, while our true self is one of love and compassion, this self is grounded in God as the source of our being; see James Finley, *Merton's Palace of Nowhere* (Notre Dame, IN: Ave Maria Press, 1978).

2. J. Francis Stroud, SJ, *Praying Naked*, 54.

3. Thich Nhat Hanh, *The Miracle of Mindfulness: An Introduction to the Practice of Meditation* (Boston: Beacon Press, 1999).

4. Anthony de Mello, *Awareness: The Perils and Opportunities of Reality* (New York: Image Books, 1990).

5. Schwartz, *Internal Family Systems* and *Introduction to Internal Family Systems*.

6. Marshall B. Rosenberg, *Nonviolent Communication: A Language of Life* (Encinitas, CA: PuddleDancer Press, 2003), 16–66.

7. Coleman Barks, trans., *The Essential Rumi* (San Francisco: HarperSanFrancisco, 1995), 109.

8. The Welcoming Presence Meditation has similarities to Buddhist practices of mindfulness described, for example, in Hanh's *The Miracle of Mindfulness* and Mary Mrozowski's practice popularly known as the "Welcoming Prayer" taught by Thomas Keating and described in Cynthia Bourgeault's *Centering Prayer and Inner Awakening* (Lanham, MA: Cowley Publications, 2004), 135–52. The essential difference is that the Welcoming Presence Meditation does not "let go" of interior movements but allows them to remain in one's interior space as guests.

Chapter 4: Taking Their PULSE

1. Elizabeth A. Johnson, *She Who Is: The Mystery of God in Feminist Theological Discourse* (New York: Crossroad Publishing Company, 1994), 260.

Chapter 5: Deciding What to Do

1. For the wording of this translation, see Walter Wink, *Engaging the Powers: Discernment and Resistance in a World of Domination* (Minneapolis, MN: Fortress Press, 1992) 186.

2. For these interpretations, see Wink, *Engaging the Powers*, 175–84, and Walter Wink, *The Powers That Be: Theology for a New Millennium* (New York: Doubleday, 1998), 98–111.

3. Wink, *Engaging the Powers*, 177.

4. "That's How I Like to See a Woman" by Sue Monk Kidd, excerpted from *The Dance of the Dissident Daughter: A Woman's Journey from Christian Tradition to the Sacred Feminine* (New York: HarperCollins, 1996), 7–10. Reprinted in Laura Slattery et. al., eds., *Engage: Exploring Nonviolent Living* (Oakland, CA: Pace e Bene Press, 2005), 20–21.

5. For an inspiring documentary chronicling this campaign, see "We Were Warriors," *A Force More Powerful*, directed by Steve York et al. (Princeton, NJ: Films for the Humanities and Sciences, 2000), DVD.

6. Paul Tullis, "Can Forgiveness Play a Role in Criminal Justice," *New York Times Magazine*, January 4, 2013: http://www.nytimes.com/2013/01/06/magazine/can-forgiveness-play-a-role-in-criminal-justice.html?_r=0). For a helpful primer on restorative justice, see Howard Zehr, *The Little Book of Restorative Justice* (Intercourse, PA: Good Books, 2002).

7. Frederick Buechner, *Wishful Thinking: A Theological ABC* (San Francisco: Harper & Row, 1973), 95.

8. For contact information on the Batkid Fund, see https://sf49ers.ejoinme.org/?tabid=504688.

Recommended by

The Academy
for spiritual Formation®
THE UPPER ROOM

For those who hunger for deep spiritual experience . . .

The Academy for Spiritual Formation® is an experience of disciplined Christian community emphasizing holistic spirituality—nurturing body, mind, and spirit. The program, a ministry of The Upper Room®, is ecumenical in nature and meant for all those who hunger for a deeper relationship with God, including both lay and clergy. Each Academy fosters spiritual rhythms—of study and prayer, silence and liturgy, solitude and relationship, rest and exercise. With offerings of both Two-Year and Five-Day models, Academy participants rediscover Christianity's rich spiritual heritage through worship, learning, and fellowship. The Academy's commitment to an authentic spirituality promotes balance, inner and outer peace, holy living and justice living—God's shalom.

Faculty trained in the wide breadth of Christian spirituality and practice provide content and guidance at each session of The Academy. Academy faculty presenters come from seminaries, monasteries, spiritual direction ministries, and pastoral ministries or other settings and are from a variety of traditions. Frank Rogers is on the list of faculty for The Academy and currently serves on The Academy Advisory Board.

The ACADEMY RECOMMENDS program seeks to highlight content that aligns with the Academy's mission to provide resources and settings where pilgrims encounter the teachings, sustaining practices, and rhythms that foster attentiveness to God's Spirit and therefore help spiritual leaders embody Christ's presence in the world.

Learn more here: http://academy.upperroom.org/.